GREAT AMERICAN THINKERS

Alexander Hamilton

The First Secretary of the Treasury and an Author of the Federalist Papers

Tatiana Ryckman

Cavendish Square

New York

Published in 2017 by Cavendish Square Publishing, LLC
243 5th Avenue, Suite 136, New York, NY 10016

Library of Congress Cataloging-in-Publication Data

Names: Ryckman, Tatiana, author.
Title: Alexander Hamilton : The First Secretary of the Treasury and an Author of
the Federalist Papers / Tatiana Ryckman.
Description: New York : Cavendish Square Publishing, 2016. | Series: Great
American thinkers | Includes bibliographical references and index.
Identifiers: LCCN 2016007068 (print) | LCCN 2016008137 (ebook) |
ISBN 9781502619341 (library bound) | ISBN 9781502619358 (ebook)
Subjects: LCSH: Hamilton, Alexander, 1757-1804--Juvenile literature. |
Statesmen--United States--Biography--Juvenile literature. | United
States--Politics and government--1783-1809--Juvenile literature.
Classification: LCC E302.6.H2 R93 2016 (print) | LCC E302.6.H2 (ebook) |
DDC 973.4092--dc23
LC record available at http://lccn.loc.gov/2016007068

Editorial Director: David McNamara
Editor: Elizabeth Schmermund
Copy Editor: Rebecca Rohan
Art Director: Jeffrey Talbot
Designer: Amy Greenan
Production Assistant: Karol Szymczuk
Photo Research: J8 Media

CONTENTS

INTRODUCTION

Sharp Wit and Financial Savvy

A lexander Hamilton moved to America at one of the most exciting times in the nation's history—its founding.

In 1773, a big change was on the horizon for colonial America. Colonists were enraged by taxation without representation, and Britain was equally frustrated by its unruly American subjects. Even as the revolution was underway, many colonists believed they were fighting for representation in British Parliament, not independence from their motherland.

Though he was only a teenager when he arrived in New York from the **West Indies**, Hamilton quickly became a prominent supporter of a new, independent government. Even while he was still a student in New York, he penned public letters in support

One of the earliest known portraits of Hamilton, this painting by Alonzo Chappel depicts the young soldier in the uniform of the New York Artillery.

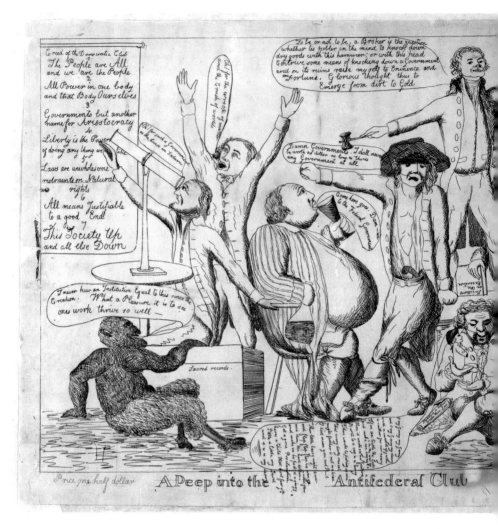

of the **Continental Congress,** the first body of representatives from across the colonies. He gained notoriety for his sharp writing and financial savvy.

Hamilton's legacy has been honored with his portrait on the ten-dollar bill. That honor was bestowed upon him for his ardent defense of the Constitution while a new America sought its identity and the form its government would take. It was no secret that the revolution

Fierce opponents of Alexander Hamilton, Antifederalists fought for minimal government control. This political cartoon, "A Peep into the Antifederal Club," mocks the party by placing its leader, Thomas Jefferson, alongside the devil and a drunkard.

had drained the nation's funds and that the new country's debts ran deep. In the face of public fear about abuse of powers, Hamilton repeatedly argued for a national government with the right to tax.

Together with James Madison, who authored the Constitution, and John Jay, a prominent member of the New York **Committee of Correspondence**, Hamilton authored many of the *Federalist Papers*. These essays were published in response to opposition to the Constitution and encouraged states to support a strong federal government.

After convincing American citizens, as well as the Congress, that a strong centralized government was in the best interest of the people, Hamilton remained deeply loyal to his cause. After being appointed secretary of treasury by President George Washington, Hamilton issued his first report on the country's economic affairs. Still suffering from the chaos of war, Hamilton began advocating for a national bank that would take on states' individual debts to help win their trust.

Despite much resistance from a few wealthy states, Hamilton's proposal for a national bank was passed.

Alexander Hamilton's views were not always popular, and his sharp tongue sometimes got him into trouble. Still, he persists in the collective memory of his country for his dogged defense of liberty and unity in a fledgling United States.

CHAPTER ONE

The Dawn of Independence

L eading up to the American Revolution were a number of events, both civil and religious, that encouraged early Americans to rebel against their far-off British rulers. From the beginning, America was a melting pot of culture with immigrants from England, France, Spain, Sweden, and the Netherlands establishing settlements along its eastern coast. Slowly, Britain took control of the settlements scattered across the thirteen new colonies and **assimilated** those populations, encouraging settlers from other countries to become subjects of England.

Early American Colonization

The dominant opinion throughout much of Europe in the seventeenth and eighteenth centuries—held by both Catholics and Protestants alike—was that there was only one correct

Far from the Manhattan we know today, this woodcut shows early Dutch colonists arriving on Manhattan Island.

religion, and that it was the government's obligation to enforce God's intentions. It was this climate of **intolerance**, or unwillingness to accept the views of others, that led many people to leave their homes and families to settle in the new, distant American colonies. But religion was not the only motivation for newcomers. Early America offered the promise of untouched wealth, unclaimed land, and adventure.

In order to capitalize on the wealth of this new land, Britain also established **mercantilism**, a policy that created partnerships between merchants and the English government to help funnel America's prosperity back to the homeland, often to the exclusion of other nations and England's own colonies. When American merchants traded with other nations, the British government considered this **smuggling**, or illegal trading, and those merchants were punished as if they'd stolen from Britain.

The Foundation of the American Revolution

Murmurings of dissent from the colonists began as early as 1754. That May, **Benjamin Franklin**, inventor, publisher, politician, and one of the Founding Fathers, published a famous political cartoon titled "Join, or Die" in the *Pennsylvania Gazette*. In this image, a segmented snake (each segment representing a different part of the early colonies) slithers across the panel.

"Join, or Die" accompanied an editorial by Franklin about the disconnected state of the colonies. At that time, the colonies were less concerned with British domination and worried instead about the threat of Native Americans and their French allies. Settlers sought to expand west, beyond the Appalachian Mountains, in search of more land and natural resources. The French and certain Native American tribes united against that expansion, leading to the **French and Indian War** (a conflict named for its allies, rather than the two sides of the disagreement). Over time, this same cartoon was used to unite the colonists against the authoritarian rule of the British, and it was revived again during the American Civil War.

In May 1754, Benjamin Franklin published this famous political cartoon, "Join, or Die," in the *Pennsylvania Gazette*. The segmented snake represents the early colonies and boldly declares the need for unity among the divided colonies.

In Franklin's accompanying editorial, he praised the **Albany Plan**, which recommended uniting the colonies. He wrote that the unification of the colonies was necessary, and stated:

> The Confidence of the French in this Undertaking seems well-grounded on the present disunited State of the British Colonies, and the extreme Difficulty of bringing so many different Governments and Assemblies to agree in any speedy and effectual Measures for our common defense and Security; while our Enemies have the very great Advantage of being under one.

The Albany Plan would have unified the colonies in their relations to the Native Americans and French, allowed the new government to collect taxes to support itself, and given colonists an avenue by which to rule themselves. Initially, British officials saw the unifying of the colonies as a benefit, as it would make the new territory easier to monitor and govern, and believed America's orders would ultimately come from London.

Despite Franklin's impassioned plea, the Albany Plan never went into effect because the colonies feared increased government interference—from both other colonies and the British Parliament. It was an important document, though, as it was the first attempt to unite the colonies under one government.

Taxation without Representation

Britain began to experience financial hardship as a result of the **Seven Years' War**, the larger war between European countries and their colonial empires, of which the French and Indian War was a part. As a result, the British government passed new laws and taxes for the American colonists. In 1764, the British Parliament passed the **Quartering Act**, demanding colonists feed and house British soldiers. This was especially frustrating to the colonists because British soldiers were rarely well behaved. Because the army was voluntary, British soldiers who came to America were sometimes criminals who had been recruited from the gallows. It was not uncommon for a judge to give a prisoner the choice between the noose and the navy.

Tensions between colonists and British soldiers, whom colonists referred to as "regulars," were further heighted as regulars took odd jobs to make money in order to supplement their volunteer service. There were few jobs available, and early Americans worried that they would lose them to the soldiers that the colonists also had to feed and house.

The British also levied new taxes in 1765 through the **Stamp Act**, which charged a tariff on common goods like sugar and printed materials. The new revenue was intended to pay for the British military's stay in America, ostensibly to defend the colonists against the French and Native Americans. However, as far as the colonists could tell, especially the residents of Boston, the standing army did little more than invite criminals into their homes to spy on them.

Although they paid less in taxes than their brethren back in England, the colonists were outraged at being taxed without first being asked. They took to the street to protest "taxation without representation," that is, taxation by a government in which they were unable to take part. As a result, American merchants and colonists boycotted the taxed goods. To further complicate matters, British Parliament passed the **Currency Act**, forbidding colonies from issuing new paper money, which made it even more difficult for colonists to pay debts and taxes.

By the 1760s, Europeans had been moving to this new land of opportunity for over one hundred years; fighting government, economic, and religious hierarchy was a part of their cultural education, and their tolerance for further oppression was low. Furthermore, the population of the colonies was staggeringly young—50 percent of the population was under fifteen years old. These young Americans grew up with a rebellious spirit that they passed on to future generations.

Evidence of Unrest

The colonists took their protests seriously and organized elaborate acts that would directly affect the British government. The protesters gained the attention they sought when they boycotted British cloth. Anyone found wearing British wool would be tarred and feathered, an act that was not just embarrassing but harmful. This was also usually accompanied by a brutal beating. The women of the colonies had to act fast, spinning wool to make new clothes so their families would not be taken for British sympathizers.

By 1766, the boycott had the intended effect, and British Parliament repealed the Stamp Act.

Angry colonists protested the Tea Act—taxation without representation—by disguising themselves as Native Americans and dumping boxes of tea into Boston's harbor. This infamous event is known at the Boston Tea Party.

Though originally opposed to this taxation, **Thomas Hutchinson**, the governor of the province of Massachusetts Bay, asked the British to send troops to Boston to help maintain order among the increasingly hostile colonists. In 1768, British troops arrived on American soil to squelch colonist revolts against taxation. Frustrated with King George III, whom colonists saw as an unsympathetic king ruling from across the Atlantic, angry colonists formed a mob to fight against British soldiers in 1770. This led to a violent response on the part of the soldiers, and five colonists died in the skirmish that became known as the **Boston Massacre**.

On December 16, 1973, the famous **Boston Tea Party** took place in an otherwise quiet Boston harbor. Despite angry protests against the **Tea Act,** a law that allowed the East India Tea Company exclusive control over the tea trade between India and the colonies, Governor Hutchinson followed the royal laws, ordering colonists to allow the British ships to port and to pay for the delivered tea. Angry at the tea monopoly that the British employed with the Tea Act, a group of 150 men disguised as Native Americans boarded three ships and dumped boxes of tea into the harbor.

The Library of Congress clarifies some misconceptions about the details of the Tea Act and the subsequent Boston Tea Party:

> The Act actually placed no new tax on tea (this was still on the books from the Townshend Duties). Instead, it gave the East India Company a virtual monopoly on selling tea in the colonies. The British assumed that colonists would welcome the lower price of tea achieved by eliminating the merchant middleman. The Tea Act, however, angered influential merchants who feared the monopoly would affect them directly. For many more colonists, the Tea Act revived passions about taxation without representation. Soon the colonists again responded with a boycott of tea. Earlier protests had involved relatively few colonists, but the tea boycott mobilized a large segment of colonial society.

News of the protest traveled from Vermont to North Carolina, and similar demonstrations were staged across the colonies. Copycat tea parties sprang up in New York, New Jersey, South Carolina, and Rhode Island.

In response to what the British considered vandalism, Parliament passed the **Coercive Acts** in 1774, shutting down the Boston harbor until their demands for reimbursement were met. The Boston Tea Party had destroyed over 300 pounds (136 kilograms) of tea by throwing it into the harbor, and the price was steep—the destroyed goods were worth approximately $28,000 (that's $848,000 when converted to today's dollar value). Colonists referred to this as the Intolerable Acts, further widening the gap between what Britain and the colonists saw as Britain's role on the American shore. While colonists were reluctant to pay, the surrounding colonies were quick to aid their Bostonian neighbors, sending them food and supplies to help them through the hard New England winter.

To further establish authority over the colonies, Parliament installed a military governor in Massachusetts, **General Thomas Gage**, who had previously fought alongside George Washington in the French and Indian War. Gage was instructed to enforce the Intolerable Acts, and his later actions would further incense the colonists against the British government.

The Colonies Unite

Despite the growing unrest, not all colonists advocated for separating from Great Britain. Some felt it was better to negotiate with Parliament and attempt to pay the debt from the Boston Tea Party, while others hoped to organize a mass boycott of goods imported from Britain. It was only a smaller, more radical group that had begun to suggest the idea of extricating themselves from the British Empire.

The First Continental Congress

With the pinch of British taxation and the expense of a potential war looming, without the ability to tax and generate revenue themselves, the colonies sought a solution to the oppressive atmosphere that was growing on the shores of the New World. Ultimately, the colonies decided that they should meet to discuss the future of their new homeland and to plan a course of action together. This meeting was called the **First Continental Congress**.

The First Continental Congress met from September 5 to October 26, 1774, in Philadelphia, Pennsylvania. The congress was made up of delegates from every colony except Georgia. Among the delegates sent to the congress from all over the colonies were two future presidents of the United States: George Washington and John Adams.

The delegates were united in their desire to work with Britain on reforms, but divided on what measures to take. Joseph Galloway, a representative from Pennsylvania, proposed the "Plan of Union of Great Britain and the Colonies," which would allow for an American congress to act as a counter to Parliament and a president general appointed by the king to act on his behalf in the colonies. This plan was very nearly passed, but as the vote approached, tensions escalated in Boston. **Paul Revere** arrived with a letter from Boston, which stated that the Bostonians would boycott British goods unless the Intolerable Acts were repealed.

Galloway suggested that the Bostonians be left to figure it out for themselves, while others proposed attacking the British before reinforcements could arrive. Neither of these ideas gained much traction. The congress ultimately voiced their support of Boston and called for Americans to support them should the British attempt to forcibly enforce the Intolerable Acts.

The interruption from Boston had another effect: it changed the congress' focus from **conciliations**, or compromises, to placing a more direct pressure on Britain. In late October, the congress declared the colonies would boycott English goods starting in December if taxation without representation was not lifted. If the British continued to deny colonists representation in their own government, the colonists would stop exports to Britain in September, 1775. Delegates also signed the **Articles of Association**, which called for a boycott of British goods across all of the colonies, and drafted a letter of grievances to King George III.

COMMITTEES OF CORRESPONDENCE

While technology during the time of the revolution may seem unsophisticated in light of modern advances, the printing press was a groundbreaking means of spreading news for early American settlements. After decades of struggling to secure their basic needs, like food and shelter, the colonists finally had a chance to think beyond their basic survival to create a form of more rapid communication.

Benjamin Franklin was especially instrumental in starting presses throughout the colonies. He began a network of presses from the Southern colonies to New England and launched the first newspaper chain. Because of this network, local newspapers and underground pamphlets circulated that addressed the colonists' concerns and spread word of British abuses around the territories.

In Massachusetts, **Samuel Adams** and **John Hancock** started the first Committee of Correspondence in 1764. Adams wrote to his contemporaries about problematic English actions as well as detailed plans for protests and boycotts, while John Hancock paid for the postage. Patriot Riders, like Paul Revere, disseminated these letters throughout Massachusetts.

The idea caught on and soon committees of correspondence popped up throughout the colonies, creating unity in the colonists' efforts against the British. By the 1770s, the committees were part of local governments and used the system to maintain colony relations. When the Boston Tea Party occurred in 1773, the committees of correspondence were instrumental in informing colonists about what had happened.

Access to information, through the development of printing presses, changed the way the colonists thought of their relationship to Britain as well as to their fellow Americans.

Little did the delegates know that this stalemate would not last until September.

The Public

Worried that some merchants might take advantage of their brethren's halt on imports, the congress nominated local government officials to enforce the embargo on British goods. These officials were tasked with inspecting customhouse books and punishing offenders by printing their names in the newspapers as enemies of American liberty.

As the delegates left the congress for their homes throughout colonial America, they were greeted with patriotic enthusiasm and respect. Some of the delegates found their journey took longer than expected due to the many invitations they received to stop and dine with supporters.

From Vermont to South Carolina, colonists felt the oppression of British rule. Most colonists did not actually want to break away from the British, but they wanted Britain to treat them as equals, and not as a faraway source of money. Just in case, though, towns throughout the colonies (especially in Massachusetts and Virginia) began training a militia of minutemen—an unofficial military that could be ready to fight with just one minute's warning.

When it came time to publish the names of anyone who did not follow the new guidelines set forth by the congress, public shaming did its job. More than convincing merchants not to accept imports, the wrath of public patriotism put fear in the hearts of anyone who might not agree with the views of the Continental Congress. Some colonists were made to apologize publicly in newspapers for expressing their opinions in private letters, while others were forced to turn over tracts that criticized the Continental Congress. Even if opposition to the revolution existed, it was not given an outlet to be discussed.

Though King George III recognized the turmoil brewing in the colonies, he refused to repeal the high tariffs placed on colonists. The British Parliament even began planning additional taxes to punish the colonists for their protests.

Alexander Hamilton: The First Secretary of the Treasury and an Author of the Federalist Papers

Across the Pond

On the other side of the Atlantic Ocean, British Parliament was facing its own turmoil, in which the Americans played only a small part. The ministry had announced in September 1774 that they would hold elections for Parliament, though elections were not supposed to happen until 1775. This political move, intended to stop any opposition candidates from taking the incumbents' places, redirected most of Britain's political attention.

General Gage realized the gravity of the situation in America and wrote to London, urging Parliament to repeal the Intolerable Acts. If they would not repeal those measures, Gage wrote, he would need considerable military assistance. As a result of this recommendation, King George III began seeking General Gage's replacement. The king recognized that more military force would be necessary, but removing the Intolerable Acts, he said, was an absurd suggestion. British heads of state encouraged Parliament to pass more punitive laws against the New England colonies, and to prepare for war.

The offer presented to the colonies was relatively simple, but coercive. Parliament would drop this tax for any colony willing to make other provisions—civil and military—for Britain. After this proposition was passed, Parliament tacked on a few other laws, including restricting New England's fishing and trade.

The Revolution Begins

In early April 1775, Gage received instructions to act quickly and forcibly. Doubting he had the necessary troops to take effective military action, Gage marched his troops toward the town of Concord to seize the gunpowder stored there. If he couldn't control the rebellious Americans, he hoped to at least stop them from controlling him.

Battle of Lexington and Concord

Gage marched his men to the neighboring towns of Lexington and Concord on April 18, 1775. He sent scouts out in the afternoon to look for any trouble, though these scouts themselves caused alarm in the villages they passed through and tipped colonists off to the approaching soldiers.

Paul Revere rode from Boston to warn John Hancock and John Adams, who were hiding in Lexington, of the approaching threat. News traveled quickly and, soon, minutemen and militia gathered to defend their towns against the British.

Though they'd traveled through the night with little rest, the British Army was ready to fight as they approached Concord. When faced with a group of roughly seventy rebels along the road, the British general ordered the Americans to put down their weapons and disperse. Facing four hundred British soldiers, the rebels backed away. But this would only be the start of the battle.

Suddenly, a shot rang out. It has long been disputed which side fired first, though depositions taken in 1775 suggest that it was the British. This first mysterious shot, however, had big consequences.

Unsure of where the shot came from, a British officer commanded his troops to fire. Though others tried to stop the ensuing gunfight, it had become too loud for commands to be heard and a second shower of bullets was sent into the crowd of rebel militia. The militia shot back, but they were too outnumbered to do much damage. The battle itself lasted only a few minutes. At its end, eight militiamen had been killed while only one British soldier was wounded.

As the regulars continued to advance, joined by fresh reserves, they were repeatedly bombarded by the American militia. Though outnumbered, the militia used their knowledge of the land and the support of their communities to their advantage. When the Americans worked together, they were able to land vicious blows to the advancing troops. Even so, these early American ranks

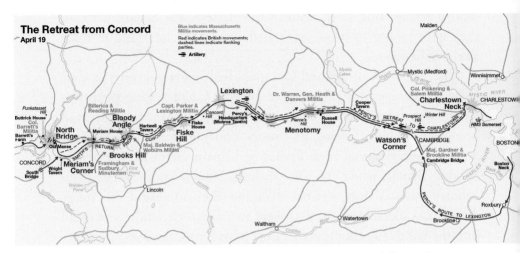

Though not a clear win for the colonists, the battles of Lexington and Concord gave the rebels hope that they might beat the British after all.

were often composed of farmers and shopkeepers, volunteers both young and old. As a result of their inexperience, the militia would often start strong as a group but chaos would give way to fighting independently, and no single rebel was a match for the strength of an army.

All along the road to Concord, militiamen struck out against the approaching regulars. Success varied from town to town, but the militia had weakened the British troops enough to bolster American confidence and instill the British with doubt. The Battles of Lexington and Concord would be the first fighting of the American Revolution.

The Second Continental Congress

The Second Continental Congress met several months after Lexington and Concord, this time with new members including Benjamin Franklin and John Hancock. Once again, the meeting focused on the problem of British forces on American soil. Due to the violence that broke out on the road to Concord, the congress knew a military was necessary and that action must be taken against

British forces. But, once again, the congress was unsure whether they were asking to break from Britain entirely or trying to force a reconciliation.

The Second Continental Congress had many concerns as they faced the choice of breaking from Britain. Chief among them was America's vulnerability against other nations. Britain's military had been spread thin, fighting in Europe and maintaining a standing army in America, and both France and Spain seemed interested in striking Britain while she was weakest. Should another European country take action against Britain—the homeland of many American colonists—colonists were worried their lands would fall into the hands of other greedy rulers from across the sea.

Another concern was whether the congress had the legislative power to form a military on behalf of the states, or if each state would be in charge of defending its own people. Influential Bostonians again sent letters to congress asking for guidance and encouraging them to build a unified military. Congress took steps to do so, appointing George Washington as military commander and approving his budget.

As the Second Continental Congress deliberated over these important steps, General Gage was looking for other ways to weaken the rebellious population. The royal governor in Virginia, for example, offered freedom to any slaves who joined Britain in combat. Over eight hundred slaves responded by joining the royal army.

Though British troops greatly outnumbered the American militia, the colonies covered such a great geographical expanse that the British were unable to take control of the American countryside. America also had a surprising asset: because each state had been largely independent from the others, there was no central city for the British army to capture.

Perhaps because of America's clear disadvantage—a small, untrained military—colonists decided to do everything they could to strengthen their ranks. Men, ranging from teenagers to the elderly, enlisted in the new military. Wealthy slave owners sent slaves to join the military in their place, with the promise of freedom at the end of the war. Women did everything from sewing and mending uniforms to taking on combat roles themselves. Conversely, the British refused the help their American supporters offered. Distrusting the Tories, or British sympathizers in the colonies, the British military turned down the sort of assistance that could have led to a stronger hold in the countryside.

Breaking Ties

Soon, the Americans realized they could not finance a war on their own. The colonists reached out to France, Spain, and Holland for aid. Benjamin Franklin, who was welcome in French courts, was instrumental in convincing the French to support the Americans against the British. This was largely due to the fact that the British and the French had been rivals since medieval times. Before the French would assist, however, they needed to know America was not planning to rejoin Britain.

Congress was now at a pivotal impasse. Would they accept French aid and break from Britain completely, or would the colonists continue to struggle to convey the seriousness of the matter to an uninterested motherland? The congress ultimately accepted French aid, and their course was set. This crucial decision led Thomas Jefferson to draft the **Declaration of Independence**, a formal, written intention of the colonies' plan to sever their political connections to Great Britain. The wording in this document was debated by delegates for many days before finally being approved on July 4, 1776.

Although he was off by several days, the future President John Adams accurately predicted the significance of that declaration in a letter to his wife, Abigail:

> The second day of July, 1776, will be the most memorable epoch in the history of America. I am apt to believe that it will be celebrated by succeeding generations as the

Though the Declaration of Independence hardly marked the end of the revolution, it did signify a new path for the American people. President John Adams correctly predicted the patriotism Americans would feel for generations to come in celebration of that momentous declaration.

great anniversary festival. It ought to be commemorated as the day of deliverance, by solemn acts of devotion to God Almighty. It ought to be solemnized with pomp and parade, with shows, games, sports, guns, bells, bonfires, and illuminations, from one end of this continent to the other, from this time forward forever more.

This was a momentous and historic occasion, but it signaled the start of a long and violent war that America would never have won without the help of its allies. Unable to pass taxes, the fledgling American government understood that support from foreign allies was the only way Americans could fight for independence. France sent ammunition, uniforms, and much-needed soldiers, while Holland contributed funds. Americans tried to print more money to pay debts, but this caused uncontrollable inflation that quickly made the continental currency worthless.

America also approached Spain about contributing to the cause of the revolution. Spain agreed to help in exchange for the American land that Britain had taken from them. Spanish aid took many forms, including sending money and supplies to the colonists. Though Spain did not send troops directly to America to fight alongside the colonists, they did join other European countries in launching their own attacks against the British, thus tying up British troops and supplies in Europe.

Foreign aid proved especially useful in the final battle of the revolution. In September 1871, the French naval fleet departed Haiti (a French colony at that time) for Chesapeake Bay. At the same time, the British chose a Chesapeake town, Yorktown, as their base. Washington led five thousand American troops to block the British from escaping by land as the French navy blocked their escape by sea. The French and Americans fired on British troops for three weeks straight until the British General, Charles Cornwallis, surrendered.

Though fighting continued on America's behalf in other parts of the world, the Battle of Yorktown marked the end of fighting within the colonies. Peace negotiations began in 1782 and the United States of America's independence was finally recognized with the signing of the Treaty of Paris in 1783. The Constitution would not follow until 1788.

American Independence

Against the odds, America was victorious. But what was America, what did it mean to be American, and who would govern these new American citizens? These were the big questions facing a new nation, alone on the other side of an ocean from the only rule they'd ever known.

CHAPTER TWO

A Personal History of Alexander Hamilton

T hough Alexander Hamilton quickly inserted himself into American politics and became known as a champion of liberty and the rights established in the Constitution, he came from the distant West Indies and experienced a turbulent childhood before coming to the North American continent.

A Complicated Youth

Hamilton claimed to be born on the island of Nevis in the **British West Indies** in 1757, but historians believe it was actually 1755. Hamilton's home life was unorthodox and marked by a series of tragedies. His mother, Rachel Faucette, left her first husband and child to take over a small estate left to her by her father.

Though an active supporter of American liberty and the Constitution, Hamilton's origins in the West Indies would lead others to treat him as an outsider through much of his career.

The West Indies are a cluster of islands between North and South America once colonized by early European settlers, just like the colonies of the United States.

Though she was still married, she moved there with James Hamilton and had two sons with him, James and Alexander.

Because his parents were unmarried, Alexander had been denied membership to the Catholic Church and, as a result, was unable to attend the local Catholic school. For a few years, though, he supplemented his own studies of the family's thirty-four books with private tutoring and a few classes at a private school.

When Alexander was still quite young his father abandoned him, his brother, and his mother. James Hamilton Sr. had learned Rachel's first husband intended to divorce her on grounds of adultery, and James left under the pretext of sparing her reputation.

Now alone, Rachel supported her family by running a modest store in Nevis's capital, Christiansted, until February 1768, when she caught a bad fever and died. Upon her death, her first husband returned to claim her estate and valuables. Some items were auctioned off, but a family friend purchased the Hamiltons' small library and returned the books to Alexander.

On His Own

Roughly ten years old, Alexander and his brother James were motherless. The brothers were taken in briefly by their cousin, but when the cousin committed suicide, they were separated. James went to apprentice with a carpenter, and Alexander was sent to work in an import-export firm where his sharp mind and eloquent language drew the attention of the proprietor and local businessmen.

Alexander's boss, a local merchant named Thomas Stevens, soon adopted him. Due to a remarkable likeness between Stevens's son and Alexander, some speculated that Stevens was Alexander's biological father, further complicating his troubled childhood. Regardless of the relation, Alexander was a part of the Stevens family and became close friends with Thomas Stevens's son, Edward.

Alexander did well at the import-export firm. He had a wide range of responsibilities and proved himself trustworthy. By 1772, Hamilton had published his first article in the *Royal Danish-American Gazette* about a hurricane that had devastated part of his home island. The community was so impressed by Hamilton's strong writing and rich vocabulary that a collection was gathered to send him to the United States for school. Many people helped fund his voyage, but his education was largely subsidized by Stevens, who would send cane sugar from the tropical island for sale in the colonies. Although Hamilton himself had no interest in working a plantation or owning slaves—he in fact fought against slavery for much of his life—his education was largely paid for by sugar produced with slave labor.

An Education

When Hamilton first arrived in the colonies, he was sent to a grammar school in Elizabethtown, New Jersey. He took quickly to his studies, working day and night and excelling at nearly every subject to which he put his mind. Hamilton was only in Elizabethtown for six months but in that short time he made invaluable connections and impressions that would color the remainder of his life—including his first introduction to Aaron Burr, who would mortally wound him many years later in a duel.

Hamilton's grammar school prepared its students to attend Presbyterian College of New Jersey, known today as Princeton. Some of Hamilton's benefactors were graduates of the prestigious school, and the elite family of his roommate, William Livingston, sat on the school's board. The school was made more appealing still by its strong focus on politics and reputation for religious freedom.

Hamilton's quick mind and impressive oratory skills won over the head of admissions, John Witherspoon. Witherspoon has been called "the most influential teacher in the entire history of American education," and indeed an exceptional number of his students went on to become senators, delegates, and even president (James Madison) and vice president (Aaron Burr). The young Hamilton possessed an enormous amount of confidence. He asked Witherspoon for permission to accelerate his studies so he could graduate sooner. This may have been when Hamilton shed those mysterious two years from his birth year. Applying at eighteen would hardly have made him look like an overachiever among the young prodigies who populated the school. Witherspoon considered Hamilton's request, but the board ultimately refused. James Madison's recent illness, after completing his bachelor's degree in just two years, may have still been too fresh in their minds.

In 1774, Hamilton enrolled at King's College, which is today known as Columbia University. King's College was more agreeable to his accelerated timeline and allowed him the unusual status of "private student" so that he would not immediately belong to any given class. Hamilton's time there overlapped briefly with Edward Stevens, his friend from the West Indies. Though the school's administration supported traditional values and sympathized with the Tories, being in New York City exposed Hamilton to the politics of the time. Living in the major trading port and political center of colonial America, Hamilton was able to see firsthand the workings of government, business, and political rebellion.

The college itself was situated between a "red light district," known for harboring all kinds of earthly temptations, and the meeting grounds for political radicals. Despite the university's strict curfew (10 p.m. in summer and 9 p.m. in winter) and the pervasive suspicion of radical thinking, Hamilton was able to make a name for himself while at King's College. With a group of close friends, Hamilton helped found a small literary and debate club. His close friend and roommate, Robert Troupe, later wrote that Hamilton's early views were loyalist and didn't stray from the ideas preached at the college. Over time, however, Hamilton came to use the debate club to air his early drafts of **revolutionary** ideology before sending them away for publication.

Soon after Hamilton started at King's College, excitement over the Boston Tea Party ignited revolutionary fervor and interrupted Hamilton's studies. He wrote articles and attended rallies, giving speeches that left his audiences rapturous. Finally, Hamilton had found an outlet for his zeal and brilliance: as a leading voice in the American Revolution.

A Moral Conviction

The American Revolution further distracted young Alexander Hamilton from his studies in 1775, when the Sons of Liberty, a group organized by colonists to fight against British rule, took a crowd to the steps of King's College with a plan to tar and feather the school's president—Hamilton's own teacher, Myles Cooper.

Hearing of the approaching mob, Hamilton went to the dormitory steps to delay them, buying the president a few valuable minutes for escape. Hamilton delivered a moving speech about virtue and fighting for personal liberties without taking them from others. Though the crowd continued into the dorms, Cooper had already escaped out of a window and over the back fence. Cooper was able to get on a ship shortly after and returned to England where he continued to rail against the American independence movement from a safe distance.

Though Hamilton disagreed with Cooper's political ideology, Cooper had served as Hamilton's mentor and offered opportunities that would have otherwise been out of reach. Proving his strong sense of honor and keen ability to separate personal relationships and politics, Hamilton risked getting a beating himself to protect his mentor and friend. This strong moral conviction and sense of integrity stayed with Hamilton his whole life.

Shortly after this rampage, King's College was taken over as a rebel military hospital and Hamilton joined the revolutionary forces, anxious to show his courage on the battlefield.

This was not the last time Hamilton would come face-to-face with an angry mob in defense of someone he disagreed with. Later that same year, Hamilton spoke to a crowd outside the shop of a Tory, or British loyalist, printer. While he maintained composure, Hamilton later wrote to his friend John Jay that, even though he disagreed with the printer, the violence of the lower classes bore a greater resemblance to anarchy than to a new, fair government. These trying times may have influenced his political ideals and led to his fear of mob rule. These concerns, however, likely contributed to what his detractors referred to as his elitism during the later drafting of the Constitution.

A Military Mind

Hamilton took to the military with the same exuberance he brought to his studies. He studied military tactics, parade exercises, and even uniforms. He was fastidious and demanded his troops look the part, lest they be ridiculed and shamed. Word of this extraordinary young captain made its way to General George Washington, who asked to see Hamilton's troops.

General George Washington's Friendship

During the brutal first battles of the revolution, Alexander Hamilton had opportunities to show off his intellectual talent and organizational skill in view of General George Washington. Though he was new to battle, Hamilton's professionalism and dedication spoke volumes to Washington, especially as his troops thinned due to casualties and deserters. Over time, the general brought Hamilton into his confidence and relied on his advice and assistance.

In December 1776, Hamilton lay ill as Washington planned the famous Battle of Trenton. Though unwell, Hamilton mustered his energy and joined his company, which had already been reduced by half after a disastrous campaign in New York. Hamilton's persistent fire gave Washington's men cover as they sneaked into the sleepy enemy encampment at Trenton and forced their captures to surrender. News of the rebels' success traveled quickly and healed the soldiers' bruised morale.

In the wake of a few small victories due to Hamilton's valiant performance as Captain, Washington promoted him to lieutenant colonel. By March 1777, Hamilton was working directly under Washington as his aide-de-camp, sensing the general's needs and thoughts before Washington could even voice them. Though Washington was an invaluable leader and a symbol to the fledgling nation, he often struggled to express himself. Hamilton's quick mind and literary aplomb became invaluable to the general as he sought the best way to explain his needs on the battlefield to members of Congress. This role inevitably led to Hamilton's deep involvement in all of Washington's most confidential and diplomatic obligations. While Hamilton's studies had been waylaid by the revolution, his vast array of responsibilities gave him remarkable training in politics and diplomacy.

ANOTHER IMPORTANT ALLIANCE

Hamilton was enlisted in the military during the first years of his twenties and, though the nation was at war, he couldn't help but notice the young women who would visit the aristocratic officers for formal balls and events between battles. Hamilton was very flirtatious and a rotating cast of young women consumed his spare moments. One woman in particular caught his eye: the young, wealthy Elizabeth Schuyler.

An orphaned foreigner, Hamilton had little to offer Elizabeth socially, but her father was close friends with General Washington and thought fondly of Hamilton. What the young soldier lacked in finances and breeding, he made up for with wit and charm. Elizabeth was also thought to be charming and down-to-earth despite her family's great wealth. After courting for only a few months, they decided to get married.

Though Elizabeth was not as engaged in Hamilton's career as some of the other leading ladies of the revolution, she was supportive and developed a close relationship with Mrs. Washington that mirrored the friendship between her husband and the soon-to-be first president.

After their wedding, Elizabeth quickly became pregnant, and the couple's first of eight children was born only a few months after the final battle of the revolution.He was named Philip, after his grandfather Schuyler.

For the rest of his life—despite the growing demands on his time—Hamilton remained a doting husband and father. All of Hamilton's surviving children (one of whom was adopted from a veteran of the war) remembered their father fondly in public and in private.

This famous portrait of George Washington shows his bedraggled troops crossing the icy Delaware River on the way to the Battle of Trenton.

Although Hamilton was disappointed to be taken out of battle, even for a promotion, the alliances he made among the military elite at this time would later form the foundation for his political support. Perhaps none of these relationships was as important as the one formed with the future first president himself. Author Ron Chernow writes in his biography of Hamilton:

> The relationship between Washington and Hamilton was so consequential in early American history—rivaled only by the intense comradery between Jefferson and Madison—that it is difficult to conceive of their careers

apart ... Washington possessed the outstanding judgment, sterling character, and clear sense of purpose needed to guide his sometimes wayward protégé ... Hamilton, in turn, contributed philosophical depth, administrative expertise, and comprehensive policy knowledge ... He could transmute ... revolutionary dreams into enduring realities. As a team, they were unbeatable and far more than the sum of their parts.

A Life of Politics

The war played an important role in encouraging citizens to see the whole of America as their country—rather than directing their allegiance to their home states. Even so, after the revolution, many new Americans questioned the role of government in their lives. While the Continental Congress had been divided on these issues throughout the revolution, those disagreements became the cornerstone of debates as the Founding Fathers worked to define a new nation and to divvy control between the states and federal government. It was Hamilton's professional goal to keep the states united and, to that end, bills he introduced to Congress invested greater and greater power in the central government.

Preludes to Greatness

Though he was one of Washington's closest advisors and had been promoted above many wealthier and better-connected officers, Hamilton was repeatedly passed over for positions in Congress as well as posts abroad. Hamilton's successes planted the seeds of resentment in other officers, who felt they should have been promoted above him, while also breeding resentment in Hamilton himself, who felt he was an untapped asset to Congress.

As the war dragged on through another dismal winter at the end of 1780, Hamilton was passed over for the position of superintendent of finance. When a wealthy merchant, Robert Morris, was elected to the post, Hamilton wrote him a thirty-one-page letter detailing his plan for America's economic recovery.

Rather than being put off by such a bold move on the part of someone so young and unknown, Morris replied that he agreed with many of Hamilton's ideas and another important alliance was made.

During this time, Hamilton began to form his thoughts on national finance based on his observations of America's **Articles of Confederation** in comparison to the governing laws of other nations, as well as the source of other countries' income and the fairness of various practices. Over the course of his career, Hamilton remained consistent to these early ideas. Rather than change his mind over time, he developed his theories and committed himself to them more ardently.

Though unable to work directly with Congress, Hamilton's military successes during the revolution led to political successes after America emerged triumphant. Hamilton's closeness with General Washington and Robert Morris, for example, eventually resulted in an appointment as secretary of the US treasury.

When the war ended, Hamilton spent two months recovering in Albany, New York, while also resuming his legal studies. Because his degree had been cut short as a result of the revolution, Hamilton was allowed to take the New York bar exam without completing his studies. He passed the exam after studying for only six months. Aaron Burr had also moved to New York to practice law, and the two men often met in personal and professional settings. They seldom disagreed politically and were able to maintain a pleasant personal acquaintance for many years.

Home in New York

The Hamiltons eventually made their home in New York City. After the last of the British were removed from the city, a parade of exuberant patriots marched in to reclaim their property. What they found there was not encouraging: trees and fences had been cut down for firewood, homes had been destroyed, and the pervasive stench of the whole British military living in limited quarters without garbage removal was omnipresent.

Naturally, Hamilton began drafting plans to rebuild one of America's greatest cities. He hoped that the city would not dabble in repairing existing buildings, but invest in large, ornate buildings that would last centuries.

This work was interrupted by his law practice. Hamilton was known for his large lung capacity and was a very convincing, and verbose, orator. He established a popular practice due to his reasonable prices and flawless integrity. By 1784, he had become famous for defending Tories. Zealous patriots wanted to see all vestiges of British rule removed from their country, including remaining British sympathizers. Defending Tories did not win him public favor, but it did provide an opportunity for him to challenge new state laws, which he said sometimes opposed the cause of American liberty.

National Conventions

In 1786, different states argued over trading rights and access to ports, and a convention was called in Annapolis, Maryland, to find a resolution that would set a precedent for the future. As a new member of the New York Assembly, Hamilton was one of six officials selected to attend the convention. Attendance to this meeting was abysmal, however, and in the end the delegates from all the colonies numbered only twelve.

The intimacy of the group may have helped the delegates find that the trade disputes were representative of issues pervasive in the Articles of Association. Hamilton's friend James Madison was there, and the two worked together to advocate for a second convention in one year's time, at which point the Articles would be revised.

One year later, Hamilton was chagrined to find that two New York opponents of federal government were accompanying him to

Though they would later be rivals, Hamilton and the future president James Madison had begun their relationship as friends and allies in the revolution.

the Constitutional Convention. New York governor George Clinton had named these delegates in order to thwart Hamilton and other **Federalists**, or supporters of a strong federal government, from gaining ground at the convention.

The Constitutional Convention was James Madison's moment of glory. While others arrived at the meeting prepared to tinker with the Articles, he proposed an entirely new document that would become the framework for the new Constitution. This Constitution would create a federal government divided across three branches: the legislative branch for making laws, the executive branch for administering laws, and the judicial branch for interpreting laws.

Of course, there was still work to be done. The Constitution had to be ratified by nine of the thirteen states. With some powerful opponents, this mandatory authorization by the colonies would prove a challenge—possibly nowhere as much as Hamilton's own New York. Thus began Hamilton and Madison's tireless work to convince Americans of the benefit of ratifying the Constitution through the *Federalist Papers*. These papers positioned both Madison and Hamilton to become important members of the new government—as long as the American people approved this new government.

Fame and Misfortune

Hamilton's enormous influence and tireless work in the name of democracy led to his appointment as secretary of the treasury. His elaborate financial plans for the country propelled it well into the future of modern finance but also gained many critics. Among them were Thomas Jefferson, James Madison, and other powerful men of the time. The quick shifting of economic power from the states to the central government was alarming to many and, as Hamilton rose to unfathomable power, his critics grew in number. His ideas met with mixed success although his policies had far-reaching implications and left a lasting mark on both the American economy and culture.

At the pinnacle of his power, Hamilton also became embroiled in the first major scandal in American history. Though otherwise fastidious in character, Hamilton was seduced by a woman in distress from an abusive relationship. He entertained this relationship while his wife and children were away, visiting Elizabeth's father in Albany. Over time it became clear to Hamilton that he had been duped by the woman into giving away delicate government information. Suddenly, she reconciled with her husband who, to Hamilton's horror, blackmailed him with threats to publicly air the affair.

In addition to these very real problems, Hamilton was sensitive to public perception and imagined his countrymen to be guilty of the basest motivations. Along with public disapproval of his taxation on spirits and other political actions, Hamilton felt he could no longer help America through his public position. Even if Hamilton had a touch of paranoia regarding his colleagues, the fear was not without foundation.

After his wife suffered a miscarriage in 1795, Hamilton informed Washington that he would be resigning from the treasury. He broke the news to his staff, saying, "So long as we are a young and virtuous people, [the Constitution] will bind us together in mutual interest, mutual welfare, and mutual happiness. But when we become old and corrupt, it will bind us no longer." Less an admission of his own moral stumble, Hamilton painted a dark future for America.

An Unfortunate End

Alexander Hamilton and Aaron Burr had a professional relationship for many years, although their personalities differed greatly. During the Revolutionary War, Burr was vigilant and cautious, while Hamilton longed for the romance of a heroic death. When they both became lawyers, Hamilton appreciated Burr's eloquence in the courtroom but questioned the logic of his arguments as well as his moral compass. As a fellow politician, Burr acknowledged Hamilton's skill as an orator and economist but resented his success.

These disagreements came to a head in 1804 when Hamilton's private remarks suggesting a lack of confidence in Burr were printed in a local paper. At a private party, Hamilton had said that he found Burr "despicable" to his host—an eavesdropping guest later wrote about these remarks in a letter to a friend. Somehow, this letter was published.

Hamilton had always been confident in his ability to negotiate resolutions. After all, his reputation was that of a first-rate orator. But Hamilton did not attempt to negotiate with Burr in the face of an impending duel. Burr wrote to confront Hamilton about the allegation three months after the conversation referenced in the newspaper occurred. Hamilton himself had never seen the paper and was not aware of the brewing conflict. When he received the note, rather than issuing an apology that might soothe Burr's animosity, he was dismissive, almost spurring Burr on. Hamilton replied:

> I can not reconcile it with propriety to make the acknowledgment or denial you desire, I will add that I deem it inadmissible on principle, to consent to be interrogated

as to the justness of the inferences which may be drawn by others, from whatever I may have said of a political opponent in the course of a fifteen years competition.

Burr took deep offense at this reply and multiple mutual friends stepped in to encourage Hamilton to offer a light apology, which they hoped would help to avoid the inevitable conflict. Yet Hamilton could not bring himself to offer a specific explanation in his defense in regard to a general accusation published in the newspaper. Rather than apologize, he belittled Burr for taking up such a petty argument.

Hamilton was fatally wounded in his duel with Aaron Burr on July 11, 1804.

Perhaps more than that, Hamilton could not bring himself to defer to someone he felt so superior to.

On July 11, on a cliff off the New Jersey shore, Alexander Hamilton dueled Aaron Burr. No one knows who fired first, but a bullet lodged itself in Hamilton's lower abdomen. Mortally injured, he died the next day.

Hamilton's Farewell

Alexander Hamilton had been fastidious in preparing for the possibility of his death. Among the parting letters he had written and his completed will was a touching note to his grief-stricken wife, Elizabeth. It is possibly the last thing this prolific writer ever composed:

> This letter, my very dear Eliza, will not be delivered to you, unless I shall first have terminated my earthly career; to begin, as I humbly hope from redeeming grace and divine mercy, a happy immortality.
>
> If it had been possible for me to have avoided the interview, my love for you and my precious children would have been alone a decisive motive. But it was not possible, without sacrifices which would have rendered me unworthy of your esteem. I need not tell you of the pangs I feel, from the idea of quitting you and exposing you to the anguish which I know you would feel. Nor could I dwell on the topic lest it should unman me.
>
> The consolations of Religion, my beloved, can alone support you; and these you have a right to enjoy. Fly to the bosom of your God and be comforted. With my last idea; I shall cherish the sweet hope of meeting you in a better world.
>
> Adieu best of wives and best of Women. Embrace all my darling Children for me.
>
> Ever yours
>
> A H

Elizabeth Schuyler, who outlived her husband by fifty years, avowed her undying devotion for her brilliant husband until her death, at age ninety-seven.

CHAPTER THREE

Friends and Foes

Alexander Hamilton lived at an exciting period of time in our nation's history, when our country was shaped by the incredible minds of capable men and women. As one of the Founding Fathers, Hamilton and his contemporaries created the world's most powerful democracy—although he didn't always get along with the other political leaders of the time.

Aaron Burr

Born into a safe and comfortable home in Newark, New Jersey, in 1756, Burr experienced a tumultuous few years of tragedy when he was still very young. When Burr was only a year old, his father died, and one year later his mother passed away, leaving Aaron and his sister, Sarah, as orphans. The two moved in with their

As the Founding Fathers debated the best policies for their new nation, allegiances and rivalries were formed even among the members of the first cabinet.

ENGRAVED BY J. SARTAIN.

Aaron Burr

Aaron Burr knew Hamilton long before their fateful duel. The two crossed paths shortly after Hamilton's arrival in the colonies and moved in the same circles as lawyers in both Albany and New York City.

grandparents, but their grandmother also passed away. The siblings eventually went to live with their uncle in Elizabeth, New Jersey.

Before his future rival, Alexander Hamilton, arrived in New Jersey, Aaron Burr had already completed rigorous studies at College of New Jersey. In the tradition of many brilliant minds, Burr had applied to attend the school at the tender age of eleven but was turned away for being too young. After two years of studying, Burr was admitted to the sophomore class, allowing him to graduate by the age of fifteen. Thus, Hamilton and Burr moved in the same circles, working and socializing together for thirty years until the fateful duel that ended Hamilton's life.

Though he is most famous for shooting Alexander Hamilton in that duel, Burr was also an accomplished lawyer and politician who was elected vice president alongside President Thomas Jefferson.

Vice President

Thomas Jefferson's opinion of Aaron Burr was not much better than Alexander Hamilton's, but he and Madison enlisted Burr to help them campaign in the election of 1800, in which Burr was running as vice president. A few of Burr's friends tried to rig the election so that he would win the presidency, which resulted in a tie between Burr and Jefferson. Hamilton used this opportunity to rally Federalist support for Jefferson, who he saw as the lesser of two evils. Eventually, Jefferson won the election.

Though Burr's reputation was less than spotless, his colleagues praised him for being fair and professional in his duties as vice president.

A Fallen Politician

During his time as vice president, Burr was accused of everything from improper relations with his daughter to accepting bribes. Due to his fallen reputation, the vice president felt pressure to regain his honor. Before the newspaper printed the damning letter against him, Burr had told a friend he was prepared to challenge the first respectable man who published anything against him. Confirming this sentiment after the duel, George Clinton said, "Burr's intention to challenge was known to a certain club ... long before it was known to Hamilton ... [T]his circumstance induced many to consider it more like an assassination than a duel."

Following Hamilton's death and an outpouring of national grief, Burr was accused of murder and his character was attacked more ferociously than Hamilton had ever done. One newspaper even published an article stating that the killer's heart must have been filled with "cinders raked from the fires of hell."

Indeed, Aaron Burr had many faults. He showed a great lack of moral judgment after the duel, which legitimized Hamilton's adamant objections to Burr. After fleeing to avoid charges of murder, Burr wrote a crass message to his daughter in South Carolina, suggesting that, "if any male friends of yours should be dying of **ennui**, recommend him to engage in a duel and courtship at the same time."

Not everyone was sad to see Hamilton go, however, and when Burr fled the northern states he found the south to be a temporary haven. Jefferson, for whom Burr had acted as vice president, invited the ousted politician to dine at his mansion and welcomed him to preside over the senate. To add insult to the deceased Hamilton, Burr bid an eloquent farewell to his life in politics only to court European governments in an attempt to thwart further westward American expansion.

The remainder of Burr's life was spent borrowing money and jumping between countries and affairs. He was even tried for plotting to take control of the western states so he could start his own empire. Shortly before he died, Burr married a wealthy widow and so thoroughly depleted her resources that she sued for divorce before their first anniversary. Her divorce was granted on September 14, 1836—the day Aaron Burr died.

Thomas Jefferson

Many of the first members of the national Congress came from Virginia, including Thomas Jefferson. Born in 1743 to a wealthy landowner, Jefferson inherited 5,000 acres (2,033 hectares) and high social standing. Though he enjoyed the same wealth and society life of his contemporaries, Jefferson was uniquely sensitive to the plight of both the poor and slaves. He wrote privately to a friend, "I have sworn upon the altar of God eternal hostility against every form of tyranny over the mind of man."

A Silent Influence

Though he rarely spoke in Congress, Jefferson was considered a masterful writer, and he authored some of the most significant documents in American history. Jefferson wrote the Declaration of Independence in 1776, and he proposed the method Congress adopted for adding new states to the Union. As the United States extended west, some proposed setting aside land (in present-day Ohio) for a separate colony where soldiers of the revolution could live as colonists. George Washington longed to see his troops rewarded for their service and supported this measure, but Jefferson finally established something the Congress agreed on as logical: each new added territory could apply for statehood and would be equal to the original thirteen colonies upon joining the Union.

In Support of Liberty

Though Jefferson was a slave owner himself, he was famously opposed to the idea of slavery. This was an unpopular stance, especially in Virginia where slave labor was relied upon to produce exports like tobacco and grain. Jefferson's bills proposing freedom for all made little headway with a Congress composed largely of wealthy slave owners. Soon after the revolution, **abolitionists** all over the republic pointed out the hypocrisy of fighting for freedom but denying it

Though Hamilton shared many of Thomas Jefferson's goals for the country, the two became rivals because their proposed methods for meeting those goals were so different.

to one part of the population. Jefferson seconded that opinion as a member of his state's government, though backed down when he joined national politics so as not to alienate himself from his fellow Virginia representatives. Perhaps another reason Jefferson held back some of his abolitionist sympathies was because he led a luxurious lifestyle that left him with a high amount of debt, and he depended on the labor of slaves to pay it off.

Jefferson was also a champion of education and the lower classes. Though he believed that the most talented citizens should receive the best education, he was also **egalitarian** in his view of how wealthy one had to be to receive an education.

The land-owning gentry of Jefferson's home state of Virginia were not interested in paying taxes to educate poor children outside of their social circles. Jefferson argued that the opportunity for learning should be available to all who planned to live in the United States, rich and poor, girls and boys alike. He suggested that all children learn basic reading, arithmetic, and history and that the most capable students be sent to a college funded in part by taxes (for poor students) and in part by tuition paid by wealthy families.

Jefferson's ideas about class and slavery were largely unpopular among members of both the state and national government. All of the delegates were white males, and the vast majority of them were born into positions of wealth and opportunity. Though Hamilton himself had risen to high standing despite his humble beginnings, he and Jefferson had a long-running conflict about the use of public assets. Hamilton felt a large government supported by the wealthy kept the government safe from the instability of the nation's economy, while Jefferson thought this approach was elitist and detrimental to most Americans.

The Third President of the United States of America

Despite their differences, Hamilton cast his vote for Jefferson when he ran against Aaron Burr for president in 1801. Hamilton made it clear that rather than supporting Jefferson, he was voting against Burr, whom he considered unfit for office. Jefferson made a number of popular decisions during his time in office, including lowering taxes, reducing the national debt, and negotiating the Louisiana Purchase with Napoleon. The very popular Louisiana Purchase extended the United States 827,000 miles (1,330,927 ha) beyond the Mississippi River and offered American settlers a new life. As open-minded as Jefferson was, this purchase ignored the many Native American tribes who called that land home and who had no idea that the land was, or even could be, bought out from under them.

James Madison

James Madison did not seem to know what his path would be until it was already underway. During his time at the Presbyterian College of New Jersey (today's Princeton), Madison began experiencing epileptic seizures. Worried by his condition and afraid to travel, he returned to his parents' Virginia plantation upon completing his degree. Depressed and without a career in mind, it was not until the revolution that he focused his intellectual fervor on the many trials that confronted America.

Father of the Constitution

Madison's contribution to the writing of the Constitution came largely from his experience writing Virginia's constitution eleven years before. While most of the delegates from states all over the Union came prepared to finesse the Articles of Confederation into working for the growing needs of the nation (primarily through the ability to generate revenue through taxation), it was James Madison who arrived with an entirely new document in hand. Madison's proposal for a new constitution was known as the Virginia Plan. Though there was much debate about the finer points, Madison's

Because he was willing to create a new document while other legislators planned to rework the existing Articles of Confederation, James Madison is known as the Father of the Constitution.

preparedness won him a major role in drafting the new Constitution, which he referenced in the fortieth essay of the *Federalist Papers*:

[The Constitution] is to be of no more consequence than the paper on which it is written, unless it be stamped with the **approbation** of those to whom it is addressed [the American people].

Though he is credited with being the Father of the Constitution, upon hearing this phrase in his own lifetime Madison responded, "This was not, like the fabled Goddess of Wisdom, the offspring of a single brain. It ought to be regarded as the work of many heads and many hands."

Indeed, many great minds contributed to the writing of the Constitution, including Benjamin Franklin. By the time the Constitutional Convention met in 1787, Franklin was in his eighties and in poor health. As a towering figure in America's history and politics, though, he could not stay away. He lacked the energy to participate in the rousing discussions with other members of the congress—many of whom were less than half his age—but he did draft a response to the proposed Constitution when it was finally written. Too weak to speak, Franklin asked James Wilson to read his jocular response aloud to the Congress:

I confess that there are several parts of this constitution which I do not at present approve, but I am not sure I shall never approve them. Having lived long, I have experienced many instances of being obliged by better Information, or fuller Consideration, to change Opinions even on important Subjects, which I once thought right, but found to be otherwise ... Thus I consent, Sir, to this Constitution because I expect no better, and because I am not sure, that it is not the best.

A Change of Heart

Though James Madison coauthored many of the *Federalist Papers* with Alexander Hamilton, he came to oppose the Federalists and Hamilton's fiscal policy. The large government for which he'd advocated began to grow in ways he could not support. Madison believed Hamilton's financial plans for the country would benefit wealthy northerners at the expense of taxpayers everywhere. Eventually, Madison came to lead the opposition against Hamilton, thus creating the Jeffersonian, or Republican, party.

When Madison joined other delegates from Virginia in Congress, he became fast friends with Hamilton's rival, Thomas Jefferson. This friendship is considered one of the most important political relationships in early American history. Madison was influential in passing Jefferson's bill on religious freedom and later acted as secretary of state when Jefferson was elected president.

The Fourth President

Madison became the fourth president of the United States in 1808 and served two industrious terms. Though the revolution had passed, tension between the United States and British forces continued and Madison caved to pressure to take military action. Thus began the War of 1812. Unprepared to fight another war, America lost several important battles, and British forces burned the White House down. Thanks to an American victory at the Battle of New Orleans, led by future president Andrew Jackson, as well as a few well-executed naval maneuvers, public opinion of America's military action remained high. The war eventually ended in a stalemate.

After his two terms were complete, Madison retired to his Virginia plantation. He remained committed to the cause of freedom and to strengthening the union of the United States. Before his death in 1836, Madison wrote to a friend, "The advice nearest to my heart and deepest in my convictions is that the Union of the States be cherished and perpetuated."

LASTING INFLUENCE OF THOMAS PAINE'S "COMMON SENSE"

Thomas Paine is best known for his revolutionary pamphlet, **"Common Sense,"** which challenged British authority and encouraged the American colonies to declare independence. Today, the term revolutionary has a positive connotation, implying someone who can forge new ideas unfettered by tradition and popular opinion. Yet, for Paine, refusing to yield to popular opinion made many of his contemporaries view him as dangerous—even if they agreed with him.

Regardless of whether or not everyone agreed with his ideas, *everyone* read the pamphlet. People read it aloud in taverns, and General George Washington ordered it be read to his exhausted men before the battle at Trenton. Part of the essay's success was due to Paine's clear and simple language—a rare stylistic choice among his contemporaries. "Common Sense" is often given credit for rallying rebel support and uniting the colonies against Britain. In one of the pamphlet's most famous passages, Paine writes:

> To the evil of monarchy we have added that of hereditary succession ... For all men being originally equals, no one by birth could have a right to set up his own family in perpetual preference to all others for ever, and tho' himself might deserve some decent degree of honours of his contemporaries, yet his descendants might be far too unworthy to inherit them.

> Admitting that we were all of English descent, what does it amount to? Nothing. Britain, being now an open enemy, extinguishes every other name and title: and to say that reconciliation is our duty, is truly farcical. The first king of England, of the present line (William the Conqueror) was a Frenchman, and half the peers of England are descendants from the same country; wherefore, by the same method of reasoning, England ought to be governed by France.

Thomas Paine's revolutionary pamphlet, "Common Sense," is credited with uniting the colonies against Britain—Paine's own homeland. A champion of freedom for all, without regard to race or religion, Paine's essays would eventually earn him more rivals than allies.

I am not induced by motives of pride, party, or resentment to espouse the doctrine of separation and independence; I am clearly, positively, and conscientiously persuaded that it is the true interest of this continent to be so; that every thing short of *that* is mere patchwork, that it can afford no lasting felicity, — that it is leaving the sword to our children, and shrinking back at a time, when, a little more, a little farther, would have rendered this continent the glory of the earth.

CHAPTER FOUR

The Important Work of a Prolific Politician

Alexander Hamilton began to voice his thoughts on the revolution while still a student at King's College and is considered to be the most prolific writer among the Founding Fathers. His first pamphlet, "A Full Vindication of the Measures of Congress," was published in 1774, only one year after his arrival in the colonies. Hamilton's collaboration with James Madison and John Jay on the *Federalist Papers* was integral to the ratification of the Constitution. Even after Hamilton left public office, he continued to write essays confronting the issues of his time.

> Hamilton is known for his massive contribution to the American government through his political and ideological writings, though it can also be argued that he didn't know when to stop.

Hamilton's busy pen made a lasting effect on the growth of a young nation, but it also often got him in trouble.

A Full Vindication of the Measures of Congress

Though he studied under Loyalist professors and lived in a city sympathetic to British rule, Hamilton made a name for himself for his opposition to the crown. His first major publication, "A Full Vindication of the Measures of Congress," railed against naysayers to the Continental Congress' Declaration of Rights, which included a colonial bill of rights and listed the American's grievances against the British government.

Around this time, Myles Cooper, the president of King's College, began to publish well-circulated tracts in support of England, shaming the colonists for bad behavior. Though many colonists wished to see the confrontation with Britain end peacefully, Cooper's claim that British subjects were among the happiest people on earth rang false to most readers. Cooper's friend and fellow loyalist, Samuel Seabury, published his own scathing pamphlet under the name "A Westchester Farmer."

Outraged by the slander in these essays, Hamilton's new cohort of rebel friends, the Sons of Liberty, threatened to burn the pamphlet in their public response. In some instances, the document was actually tarred, feathered, and stuck to whipping posts. The possibility of conflict attracted Hamilton, as it would his whole life, and he thus wrote and published "A Full Vindication of the Measures of Congress" in response to Seabury's essays. The ideas espoused in this early work would become staples of Hamilton's ideology over his career in law, politics, and finance:

> Let me ask [opponents of the revolution], Whence arises that violent antipathy they seem to entertain, not only to the natural rights of mankind, but to common-sense and common modesty? ... they endeavor to persuade

us that the absolute sovereignty of Parliament does not imply our absolute slavery; that it is a Christian duty to submit to be plundered of all we have, merely because some of our fellow-subjects are wicked enough to require it of us; that slavery, so far from being a great evil, is a great blessing; and even that our contest with Britain is founded entirely upon the petty duty of three pence per pound on East India tea, whereas the whole world knows it is built upon this interesting question, whether the inhabitants of Great Britain have a right to dispose of the lives and properties of the inhabitants of America, or not ...

You are told, the schemes of our Congress will ruin you. You are told, they have not considered your interest; but have neglected or betrayed you. It is endeavored to make you look upon some of the wisest and best men in America as rogues and rebels. What will not wicked men attempt! ... All I ask is that you will judge for *yourselves*. I don't desire you to take my opinion, nor any man's opinion, as the guide of your actions. Our representatives in General Assembly cannot take any wiser or better course to settle our differences than our representatives in the Continental Congress have taken. If you join with the rest of America in the same common measure, you will be sure to preserve your liberties inviolate, but if you separate from them, and seek for redress alone, and unseconded, you will certainly fall a prey to your enemies, and repent your folly as long as you live.

Seabury attacked the anonymous writer with gusto in his response to "A Full Vindication." But this rebuttal only gave Hamilton time to grow in his political knowledge and opinion. Hamilton had been insulted and again turned to his pen. In reply, he wrote an unexpected eighty-page response titled "The Farmer Refuted." This tract demolished Seabury's argument. Beyond mere insults, Hamilton showed great strategic acumen in his analysis of Britain's disadvantage against an American military. Though Britain boasted a larger military force, he predicted, other European nations would come to America's aid, and the natural features of the land— familiar to Americans who had recently fought there against the French and Indians—would work in their favor.

Hamilton's success was born both of his immense skill as a writer and speaker, and of the simple fact that he was not alone in his frustration with British authority.

Off the Page

Even when his words did not touch paper, Hamilton demanded attention. Whether as a student at King's College, an aide to General Washington, Congressman, lawyer, or secretary of the treasury, Hamilton had influence. He was bright, genteel and, though slight of frame, commanded a room with ease.

Practicing Law

After the war, Tories fled America for Canada in fear of losing their lives and possessions. For years after the conflict with Britain, Tory lawyers were barred from practicing in the colonies, making way for a flood of young, eager Patriot lawyers.

As a lawyer, Hamilton was known for his skill, integrity, and stunningly low prices. He refused to work for more than he thought a case was worth and encouraged civil settlements over expensive lawsuits. Many of his contemporaries noted Hamilton's apparent lack of interest in money—he once accepted a barrel of ham as payment. That said, Hamilton knew that his true calling was to be a Congressman, and he did not shy away from opportunities to highlight his political skill. In service of his aspirations, Hamilton also took cases that would set a precedent for congressional law and understanding. It was through such cases that Hamilton was able to both think through the repercussions of the government he advocated for as well as to establish legal norms.

This included taking on cases *defending* Tories. Reviled by their patriot neighbors, Loyalists were punished repeatedly by citizens and states alike. New York, for example, passed the Trespass Act, which allowed patriots to sue Loyalists who had occupied or destroyed their property during the war. Defending the enemy did not gain Hamilton popularity, but biographer Ron Chernow writes of Hamilton's motivation for taking such cases:

> He thought America's character would be defined by how it treated its vanquished enemies … He also maintained that the nation's survival depended upon support from its propertied class, which was being hounded, spat upon, and booted from New York … He railed against the baleful precedent that would be set if the legislator exiled an entire category of people without hearings or trials.

As with enslaving people based on race, Hamilton noted that treating a group of people differently based on class or political ideology would mean that no one was safe. If the American government followed this path, it would only be a matter of time before citizens were thrown from the republic—and Hamilton believed that liberty had to be equally available to all.

The *Federalist Papers*

The public, and many Founding Fathers, grew wary as the United States faced the daunting task of developing their new government. They were afraid of building a large national power that might come to resemble British rule. In order to ease these fears, Alexander Hamilton penned his most remembered work: fifty-one of the

the means of defending ourfelves againft the ambition and jealoufy of each other.

This is an idea not fuperficial nor futile, but folid and weighty. It deferves the moft ferious and mature confideration of every prudent and honeft man of whatever party. If fuch men will make a firm and folemn paufe, and meditate difpaffionately on the importance of this interefting idea, if they will contemplate it, in all its attitudes, and trace it to all its confequences, they will not hefitate to part with trivial objections to a conftitution, the rejection of which would in all probability put a final period to the union. The airy phantoms that flit before the diftempered imaginations of fome of its adverfaries, would quickly give place to the more fubftantial profpects of dangers real, certain, and formidable.

PUBLIUS.

NUMBER IX. *A. H*

The Utility of the Union as a Safeguard againft domeftic Faction and Infurrection.

A Firm union will be of the utmoft moment to the peace and liberty of the ftates as a barrier againft domeftic faction and infurrection. It is impoffible to read the hiftory of the petty republics of Greece and Italy, without feeling fenfations of horror and difguft at the diftractions with which they were continually agitated, and at the rapid fucceffion of revolutions, by which they were kept in a ftate of perpetual vibration, between the extremes of tyranny and anarchy. If they exhibit occafional calms, thefe only ferve as fhortlived contrafts to the furious ftorms that are to fucceed. If now and then intervals of felicity open themfelves to view, we behold them with a mixture of regret arifing from the reflection, that the

the pleafing fcenes before us are foon to be overwhelmed by the tempeftuous waves of fedition and party rage. If momentary rays of glory break forth from the gloom, while they dazzle us with a tranfient and fleeting brilliancy, they at the fame time admonifh us to lament that the vices of government fhould pervert the direction and tarnifh the luftre of thofe bright talents and exalted endowments, for which the favoured foils, that produced them, have been fo juftly celebrated.

From the diforders that diffigure the annals of thofe republics, the advocates of defpotifm have drawn arguments, not only againft the forms of republican government, but againft the very principles of civil liberty. They have decried all free government, as inconfiftent with the order of fociety, and have indulged themfelves in malicious exultation over its friends and partizans. Happily for mankind, ftupendous fabrics reared on the bafis of liberty, which have flourifhed for ages, have in a few glorious inftances refuted their gloomy fophifms. And, I truft, America will be the broad and folid foundation of other edifices not lefs magnificent, which will be equally permanent monuments of their errors.

But it is not to be denied that the portraits they have fketched of republican government, were too juft copies of the originals from which they were taken. If it had been found impracticable, to have devifed models of a more perfect ftructure, the enlightened friends to liberty would have been obliged to abandon the caufe of that fpecies of government as indefenfible. The fcience of politics, however, like moft other fciences, has received great improvement. The efficacy of various principles is now well underftood, which were either not known at all, or imperfectly known to the antients. The regular diftribution of power into diftinct departments—the introduction of legiflative ballances and checks—the inftitution of courts compofed of judges, holding their offices during good behaviour

---

To gain public support for the new government, Hamilton wrote 51 of the 85 essays in the famed *Federalist Papers*.

eighty-five essays that make up the *Federalist Papers*. Published under the pseudonym "Publius," these essays argued in support of a strong national government. Hamilton's colleagues, James Madison and John Jay, wrote twenty-nine and five essays respectively. Though their collaboration was short-lived, Hamilton could hardly ask for a better ally than Madison, who had already drafted the constitution for his own state of Virginia and eventually brought that experience to Congress. Through these essays, Madison and Hamilton put their brilliance to work, dispelling myths that a unified government would inherently be a cruel monarchy and clarifying the intent of the Constitution.

Opening Remarks

In the introduction, Hamilton accused the Constitution's objectors of harboring selfish interests, writing, "dangerous ambition more often lurks behind the **specious** mask of zeal for the rights of the people than under the forbidding appearance of zeal for the firmness and efficiency of government." The idea that what is best for the populace is not always popular would come to define his work as secretary of treasury.

In Hamilton's first essay in the *Federalist Papers*, he entreated American citizens to consider the weight of the Constitution and the significance of it in American history:

> AFTER an unequivocal experience of the inefficiency of the subsisting federal government, you are called upon to deliberate on a new Constitution for the United States of America. The subject speaks its own importance; comprehending in its consequences nothing less than the existence of the UNION, the safety and welfare of the parts of which it is composed, the fate of an empire in many respects the most interesting in the world ... a wrong election of the part we shall act may, in this view, deserve to be considered as the general misfortune of mankind.
>
> Among the most formidable of the obstacles which the new Constitution will have to encounter may readily be distinguished the obvious interest of a certain class of men in every State to resist all changes which may hazard a diminution of the power, emolument [salary], and consequence of the offices they hold under the State

THE BIRTH OF PUBLIUS

In addition to writing, Hamilton read widely. His oft-used pseudonym, Publius, was inspired by works he read while under the command of General George Washington. Chief among these was Plutarch's *Lives of the Noble Greeks and Romans*, in which Publius Valerius heroically establishes a republican government after the overthrow of a tyrant.

As early as 1778—nearly a decade before the pseudonym was used for the *Federalist Papers*—Hamilton employed the name while writing a series of letters condemning former member of the Continental Congress, Samuel Chase. Chase had been accused of insider trading and cornering the flour market. There is little remaining evidence to support this accusation, but his contemporaries were convinced of his guilt, and Hamilton's disgust is apparent in these early letters. He writes to Chase:

> To form useful alliances abroad—to establish a wise government at home—to improve the internal resources and finances of the nation—would be the generous objects of [a delegate's] care ... Anxious for the permanent power and prosperity of the state, he would labor to perpetuate the union and harmony of the several parts. He would not meanly court a temporary importance by patronizing the narrow views of local interest ... he would prove the extent of his capacity by foreseeing evils, and contriving expedients to prevent or remedy them ...

> Your career has held out as long as you could have hoped. It is time you should cease to personate the fictitious character you have assumed, and appear what you really are. Lay aside the mask of patriotism, and assert your station among the honorable tribe of speculators and projectors.

The letters also show Hamilton's occasional impulse to go overboard in his critique of his colleagues. This tendency would invite conflict throughout his life and ultimately end it.

establishments; and the perverted ambition of another class of men, who will either hope to aggrandize themselves by the confusions of their country, or will flatter themselves with fairer prospects of elevation from the subdivision of the empire into several partial confederacies than from its union under one government.

Hamilton warned that some of the Constitution's most vocal detractors would have less than noble motivations for defeating this important document. As for himself, Hamilton truly believed that not ratifying the Constitution would lead to insecurity, anarchy, and "the general misfortune of mankind."

The *Federalist Papers*, Numbers Eleven Through Thirteen

In essays eleven to thirteen of the *Federalist Papers*, Hamilton hinted at his plans for the nation's finances. In particular, he wrote about the importance of revenues and the unrealized potential of an enterprising country.

In essay twelve, Hamilton writes:

> A nation cannot long exist without revenues. Destitute of this essential support, it must resign its independence, and sink into the degraded condition of a province … Nothing can be more evident than that the thirteen States will be able to support a national government better than one half, or one third, or any number less than the whole. This reflection must have great weight in obviating that objection to the proposed plan, which is founded on the principle of expense; an objection, however, which, when we come to take a nearer view of it, will appear in every light to stand on mistaken ground.

Very quickly on the heels of essay twelve, Hamilton wrote his next essay, where he imagined the financial nightmare of a divided union:

> As CONNECTED with the subject of revenue ... The money saved from one object may be usefully applied to another, and there will be so much the less to be drawn from the pockets of the people. If the States are united under one government, there will be but one national civil list to support; if they are divided into several confederacies, there will be as many different national civil lists to be provided for—and each of them, as to the principal departments, coextensive with that which would be necessary for a government of the whole. The entire separation of the States into thirteen unconnected sovereignties is a project too extravagant and too replete with danger to have many advocates.

For Hamilton, resting thirteen separate territories instead of uniting under the Constitution was based on senseless fear. In fact, there were no benefits to remaining separate—and the safety of the American people themselves depended on uniting.

The *Federalist Papers,* Number Fifteen

One of Hamilton's greatest fears—should the constitution not be ratified—was that democratic rule would devolve into anarchy. Hamilton spoke out against squandering the freedom gained in the revolution by allowing a dictator to rise to power because the people could not agree to the tenants of a democracy. These ideas are most pronounced in the fifteenth essay of the *Federalist Papers*:

> Something is necessary to be done to rescue us from impending anarchy. The facts that support this opinion are no longer objects of speculation. They have forced

themselves upon the sensibility of the people at large, and have at length extorted from those, whose mistaken policy has had the principal share in precipitating the extremity at which we are arrived, a reluctant confession of the reality of those defects in the scheme of our federal government, which have been long pointed out and regretted by the intelligent friends of the Union ...

Government implies the power of making laws. It is essential to the idea of a law, that it be attended with a sanction; or, in other words, a penalty or punishment for disobedience. If there be no penalty annexed to disobedience, the resolutions or commands which pretend to be laws will, in fact, amount to nothing more than advice or recommendation. This penalty, whatever it may be, can only be inflicted in two ways: by the agency of the courts and ministers of justice, or by military force; by the COERCION of the magistracy, or by the COERCION of arms. The first kind can evidently apply only to men; the last kind must of necessity, be employed against bodies politic, or communities, or States. It is evident that there is no process of a court by which the observance of the laws can, in the last resort, be enforced.

Hamilton closed the final essay of the *Federalist Papers* with a note of hope, writing, "The establishment of a constitution in [a] time of profound peace by the voluntary consent of a whole people is a prodigy, to the complexion of which I look forward with trembling anxiety."

Secretary of Treasury

One of Hamilton's most lasting contributions to the United States was his adept financial planning. Elected secretary of the treasury by his friend and colleague, President George Washington, Hamilton was up against the nation's first major economic crisis. Having gone deep into debt to fund the revolution, the country needed an economic plan aimed at restoring both funds and trust in the national government.

While still practicing law, Hamilton began a careful study of national banking. He familiarized himself with Robert Morris's Bank of North America, where Hamilton was named the American business agent when the principal shareholders had to travel abroad. Around this time, rural New Yorkers were pushing for a bank backed by purchased land that could be sold or developed, believing that a bank that loaned money would only be to the advantage of urban merchants. Hamilton rejected the idea as impractical. The benefit of a bank, he argued, was that it had liquid funds that could be drawn upon in times of emergency, and land could not be quickly made into available cash. He further hoped to alleviate part of the national currency crisis by working with gold and silver, thereby avoiding the volatile paper money issued by the states.

His first *Report on Public Credit* came in 1790 and outlined the many issues facing America's economy. In the years following the war, the value of the American dollar had plummeted to be virtually worthless, and shopkeepers could hardly keep up with the changing values of currency. To further complicate matters, shops still accepted foreign currency, so that each transaction might be made up of an assortment of currencies. Among his innovations were a proposal for a National Guard to ensure against smuggling, revised currency by printing new, uniform paper money in limited quantities to guard against inflation, taking on individual states' debt, and a national bank.

In these paragraphs of the *Report on Public Credit*, Hamilton addresses the need for a national government:

> To justify and preserve ... confidence; to promote the increasing respectability of the American name; to

answer the calls of justice; to restore landed property to its due value; to furnish new resources both to agriculture and commerce; to cement more closely the union of the states; to add to their security against foreign attack; to establish public order on the basis of an upright and liberal policy. These are the great and invaluable ends to be secured, by a proper and adequate provision, at the present period, for the support of public credit.

It ought not however to be expected, that the advantages, described as likely to result from funding the public debt, would be instantaneous. It might require some time to bring the value of stock to its natural level, and to attach to it that fixed confidence, which is necessary to its quality as money.

For Hamilton, a solid national government would not only be essential for reasons of justice and security, but also in order to fund public debt and keep the states connected. He saw a direct relationship between effective government and a stable economy and understood that a national government would secure the diverging economies of the states.

Hamilton's *Report on a National Bank*

Banks were hardly the ubiquitous standard they are today. In early America, few banks existed, and many Americans distrusted them as a holdover from British rule and a scheme by the wealthy to make the populace part with its hard-earned money. Even so, Hamilton had the support of merchants in the city, and the bank proved to be an unlikely source of bipartisan interest that attracted both Tory and Patriot businessmen. With this net of support, Hamilton was able to open a private bank in New York.

In addition to banking, Hamilton became concerned with national finance as he fought against the massive industry of slavery

74   *Alexander Hamilton: The First Secretary of the Treasury and*
      an Author of the Federalist Papers

Hamilton fought tirelessly to implement a national bank, believing it would help stabilize the country's economy. He got his wish, and the First Bank of the United States was built in Philadelphia, Pennsylvania.

and disagreements between states about import taxes. Time and again, these issues called Hamilton's attention back to the need for a strong central government that could provide laws for the entire nation, thus reducing the likelihood of individual states taking up arms against one another.

Hamilton had many plans for repairing the state of affairs through the treasury, but his most important was the installation of a national bank. Having just helped Robert Morris open a bank in New York, Hamilton argued that he had the experience necessary to pursue this controversial plan:

> A National Bank is an Institution of primary importance to the prosperous administration of the Finances, and would be of the greatest utility in the operations connected with the support of the Public Credit ... The following are among the principal advantages of a Bank ...
>
> Gold and Silver ... when deposited in Banks, to become the basis of a paper circulation ... acquire life, or, in other words, an active and productive quality ...
>
> [I]t is one of the properties of Banks to increase the active capital of a country ... The money of one individual, while he is waiting for an opportunity to employ it, by being either deposited in the Bank for safe keeping, or invested in its Stock, is in a condition to administer to the wants of others, without being put out of his own reach ... This yields an extra profit, arising from what is paid for the use of his money by others, when he could not himself make use of it; and keeps the money itself in a state of incessant activity ...
>
> Well constituted Banks ... augment in different ways, the active capital of the country. This, it is, which generates employment; which animates and expands labor and industry ...

There is nothing in the Acts of Congress, which imply an exclusive right in the institution, to which they relate, except during the term of the war. There is therefore nothing, if the public good require it, which prevents the establishment of another ... This is a strong argument for a new institution, or for a renovation of the old, to restore it to the situation in which it originally stood, in the view of the United States.

Hamilton argued that not only would a national bank help individual people yield an extra profit from interest, but that the nation would have a circulating reserve of money from which to draw when necessary. In Hamilton's view, a national bank would lead to an expanded labor force, increased industry, and a more stable economy. Furthermore, the creation of a national bank, according to Hamilton's interpretation, was an implied power of the federal government under the Constitution. Hamilton's arguments were persuasive and, on February 25, 1791, President George Washington signed the bill creating the first national bank into law.

CHAPTER FIVE

Praise and Criticism

Many of Hamilton's close friends and allies knew him to be a dedicated public servant and marveled at his limitless knowledge and aptitude. However, as many supporters as he had, Hamilton also faced many critics. Even after his service as secretary of treasury, Hamilton marveled at how horribly some of his contemporaries misinterpreted his ideas.

A Genius Refuted

In 1782, Alexander Hamilton was elected New York State's delegate to the national Congress. Upon arrival he was flummoxed by the inefficiency of the government. Congressmen were limited to short terms and, because many states wanted to maintain control, delegates sometimes didn't show up so voting quotas could not be met, or vetoed imperative national legislation.

Though lauded by many as a brilliant mind and a patriotic American, Hamilton also had a number of detractors who questioned his plans for the country as well as his motivation.

For someone who fought for a strong central government, the systems in place were excruciating. In a rare moment of confidence, Hamilton wrote to his financially savvy friend, Robert Morris, "The more I see the more I find reason for those who love this country to weep over its blindness." In spite of these laments, Hamilton found an important comrade in James Madison at his first convention in Annapolis. It would be years before they wrote the *Federalist Papers*, but this early meeting of the minds laid the foundation of an important friendship.

The Role of the *Federalist Papers*

Hamilton and Madison were pioneers on behalf of a new constitution that would grant the government the power to tax, form a military, and restructure the distribution of power within the government. In the wake of the revolution, politicians and citizens alike were wary of putting too much power in the hands of a centralized government. The country had just fought six years to escape a large government, but they'd gone broke in the process. Soldiers were demanding back pay for service, which the government had withheld for as many as six years in some cases. Remaining soldiers were threatening to defect or mutiny. Furthermore, the currency was valueless.

It was becoming clear that unification to support the poor and exhausted country was necessary to maintaining peace. It was under these dire conditions that Hamilton and Madison, with the periodic help of John Jay, set about writing some of the most influential essays of the time.

The *Federalist Papers* were a series of tracts promoting the complete overhaul of the Articles of Confederation. Composed of eighty-five essays in total, the papers responded to accusations against a central government, federal taxation, and a new constitution. The authors set out to convince the powerful state of New York to join in ratifying the Constitution.

The Response to the *Federalist Papers*

If the authors' aim was to convince residents of New York of their beliefs, they hardly met their goal. The papers were well-received by those already in favor of the new government, but dissenters argued that America was too vast a land, and that one government could not work for the whole population. Though the delegates to the Constitutional Convention had been sworn to secrecy, and the *Federalist Papers* were published anonymously, many people had heard about a speech Hamilton gave in 1787 arguing for an elective monarch with broad executive powers. This was a very unpopular position, and Hamilton's views were exaggerated and circulated among his detractors. The opposition used hearsay about his epic speech to misinterpret his words, both in the *Federalist Papers*, and later when he spoke at the New York ratifying convention.

The New York delegates met for their ratifying convention in Poughkeepsie, New York, with a strong opposition to the Constitution. Hamilton preached the document's many merits as he waited for news to arrive from other states. He knew that if the quota of nine states was already met, New York delegates would be more inclined to join in ratifying the Constitution. If they decided not to do so, however, they would be excluded from the Union. When at last word reached Hamilton that ten states had joined, including the powerful Southern state of Virginia, the meeting swung around to the Federalists' point of view.

Contention in Politics

If Hamilton's writing made enemies, his policies drew a more heated reaction. Where he had at first been a foreigner espousing ideas of equality and morality, possibly ruffling the feathers of his rivals but generally gaining support for his eloquent writing, when he was in a position of power many of his colleagues felt threatened. This was

New York governor George Clinton became a bitter rival of Hamilton and sought to thwart Hamilton's legislation and influence.

not because Hamilton was diabolical or malicious, but because he was so convinced of his own prowess and integrity. No one denied Hamilton's skill as a speaker and his quick mind, but those on the receiving end of his sharp wit never forgot it and seldom forgave.

Leading up to his work as head of the treasury, Hamilton bruised the egos of other influential politicians of his time. George Clinton was New York's governor from 1801 to 1804, during the ratification of the Constitution as well as the election of the first president. Though Hamilton had lauded Clinton's abilities during the revolution, he found him to be an ineffectual governor and often said so, and occasionally much worse, in his newspaper articles.

Leading up to the presidential election, the voting system was set up in such a way that the candidate with the most votes won the presidency, and the candidate with the second-most votes would become vice president. It was largely agreed that George Washington should be president and John Adams would be vice president. Hamilton was in support of both candidates. Yet, Hamilton worried that Adams would gain too many votes and win the presidency, and when George Clinton decided to run, Hamilton was doubly concerned. To ensure Washington received the presidency, Hamilton visited seven delegates and voiced his concerns, subtly encouraging them to vote for Washington, lest things go awry.

Naturally, when John Adams learned of Hamilton's meetings with delegates he took it as a personal offense. When Adams did become president, there was no room in his cabinet for Hamilton, and Clinton's cronies continued to decry him in published letters.

The First Secretary

Being the first secretary of the treasury had its benefits and drawbacks. Hamilton saw this undefined position as an opportunity to enact his fiscal policy for the new nation, and because every aspect of the government's operation necessitated money—both incoming revenue and outgoing payments—those policies affected everyone.

Hamilton expanded his economic vision across all areas of government, ranging from currency and taxation to foreign policy. His readiness to step into the affairs of other departments was the beginning of Jefferson's frustration with him. Hamilton gained additional critics by demanding national taxes. He understood taxes would be unpopular because they harkened back to the British Intolerable Acts, but that they were completely necessary to run the many workings of a strong, secure nation. Contrary to the fears of his contemporaries, Hamilton did not wield his power injudiciously. His plan projected that ninety percent of the government's revenues would come not from taxes, but from customs on trade. Despite fears of engaging with the former mother country, Hamilton also encouraged trade with Great Britain, and one-third of America's revenue came from that renewed relationship.

Other new members of the government, like Thomas Jefferson, who had been appointed secretary of state, saw Hamilton's willingness to cross into other departments as presumptuous and balked at his overwhelming confidence. But Jefferson also came to embody many of Hamilton's frustrations with politicians in general. Above all else, Hamilton worked to maintain his pride and honor. He refused to work at his law practice after his appointment to the treasury for fear of conflicts of interest, even though it meant a significant pay cut for his large family, and he loathed "public servants" who used their power for personal gain. Very few of the other officials followed these self-imposed guidelines, sometimes blurring the line between personal and public interest. Hamilton distrusted Jefferson, seeing him as a politician who relied on rhetoric for public approval rather than working for unpopular changes that would be to the republic's advantage.

National Debt

Hamilton also gained critics in unlikely places. His fellow Federalist writer, James Madison, grew wary of Hamilton's insistence on maintaining a national debt by assuming the states' remaining war debt, and by repaying bonds that had been sold during the war to generate much needed revenue. With inflation, the bonds had dropped to a fraction of their original value and many soldiers, still unpaid for their service, had sold their bonds at a loss. These bonds were sure to regain value as trust in the government improved.

Currency was varied throughout the United States, causing far-reaching economic problems. This threepence note printed by Benjamin Franklin and David Hall was legal tender in the state of Pennsylvania.

Madison's distrust of Hamilton's debt plan was yet another example of Hamilton's work being misinterpreted. Some went so far as to accuse him of working on behalf of the British.

While he did support maintaining national debt because it allowed the populace to invest in the government through bonds, he was also adamant that this debt could only be used to the government's advantage if those who purchased the bonds trusted the government would pay them back. Additionally, his fiscal plan included a sinking

THE ECONOMY OF SLAVERY

Many New England states did away with slavery before it was nationally abolished. The land was not conducive to producing large crops, and the Quaker history of the area may have contributed to the belief that people are all equal in the eyes of God. Because slavery was a massive business in the South, outlawing the practice had implications that extended beyond morals. In some Southern states, the slave population exceeded that of whites, and Southern politicians worried the economy of half the nation—and perhaps more significantly, their own fortunes—would be thrust into uncertainty if slavery were outlawed.

Many economists have debated the extent of economic gains slave owners may have experienced. Some argue that slaves provided a higher yield on investments than government bonds, while other argue that *money* wasn't the objective at all—it was the appearance of wealth that a large plantation suggested. Beyond the limits of personal gain, the South as a whole was economically stunted because Southerners rarely traded with each other. They would either produce what they needed themselves or buy what they couldn't get from the North.

Economists theorize that these large financial problems are what ultimately made it possible to end slavery.

fund, which would skim income from post-office revenues for the explicit purpose of paying off the national debt at the rate of 5 percent per year. In 1789, the combined national and state debt was $79 million, and Hamilton in no way supported keeping it there.

It was policies like these that led his rivals to accuse him of being elitist, creating a government by and for the wealthy aristocrats who could afford to purchase government debt. Yet, if anyone in the early government was supportive of opportunities for talented but unprivileged souls to rise through the ranks of society, it was Alexander Hamilton. Among the Founding Fathers, it was Hamilton who represented this very American struggle, and furthermore refused opportunities to become wealthy, preferring to keep his integrity intact.

Hamilton's debt plan was not without supporters, though. Roger Sherman, a member of Congress from Connecticut, outlined his support of the plan in a letter to Governor Samuel Huntington:

> The report of the Secretary [Hamilton] has been under consideration for some time respecting a provision for the national debt ... The assumption of the debts of the several states incurred for the common defense during the late war, is now under consideration. The Secretary of the Treasury has been directed to report what funds can be provided for them in case they should be assumed ... He supposed that sufficient provision may be made for the whole debt, without resorting to direct taxation, if so I think it must be an advantage to all the states, as well as to the creditors. Some have suggested that it will tend to increase the power of the federal government & lessen the importance of the state governments, but I don't see how it can operate in that manner ...
>
> I have ever been of the opinion that the governments of particular States ought to be supported in their full vigour, as the security of the civil & domestic rights of

the people more immediately depend on them ... and the principal advantages of the federal government is to protect the several States in their enjoyment of those rights, against foreign invasion, and to preserve peace, and a beneficial intercourse between each other.

Although John Adams and Alexander Hamilton had a difficult personal relationship, as a fellow Federalist Adams also championed Hamilton's plans for the federal government to take on states' debts.

National Bank

Hamilton's proposition for a national bank also drew many detractors, namely Thomas Jefferson, who saw the bank as overstepping the bounds of the Constitution.

Against Hamilton's bank bill, Jefferson wrote:

> The incorporation of a bank, and other powers assumed by this bill have not, in my opinion, been delegated to the U.S. by the Constitution ... To erect a bank, and to regulate commerce, are very different acts. He who erects a bank creates a subject of commerce in its bills: so does he who makes a bushel of wheat, or digs a dollar out of the mines. Yet neither of these persons regulates commerce thereby ... For the power given to Congress by the Constitution, does not extend to the internal regulation of the commerce of a state (that is to say of the commerce between citizen and citizen) which remains exclusively with it's own legislature; but to it's external commerce only, that is to say, it's commerce with another state, or with foreign nations or with the Indian tribes. Accordingly the bill does not propose the measure as a "regulation of trade," but as "productive of considerable advantage to trade."

The disagreement between Hamilton and Jefferson had to do with interpreting the powers set forth for the federal government in the Constitution. Jefferson believed that a strict interpretation of the Constitution was necessary, while Hamilton believed that certain powers were more loosely implied. While Hamilton eventually won this argument and his bank bill was signed into law, this debate continues in American political discourse to this day.

Outside Influence with Lasting Consequences

Hamilton was aware that his control of the nation's finances would put him under unwavering examination. As he wrote in a letter to a friend, "to every man concerned in the administration of the finances of a country … *suspicion* is ever eagle-eyed and the most innocent things are apt to be misinterpreted."

But Hamilton had no idea that he might be under additional scrutiny because of increased attention on certain societal issues. His plans for the nation were temporarily overshadowed by abolitionist petitions, demanding an end to the slave trade. Though it had not escaped anyone's attention that owning slaves was the antithesis of "freedom and liberty for all," the Southern slave owners could not be persuaded. There was too much money to be lost. To further thwart the abolitionist movement, Southern states had refused to ratify the Constitution in 1787 unless a provision be written in that slavery would be uncontested for twenty years, until 1808.

Chernow notes in his biography, *Alexander Hamilton*:

> The most damning and hypocritical critiques of [Hamilton's] allegedly aristocratic economic system emanated from the most aristocratic southern slaveholders, who deflected attention from their own nefarious deeds by posing as populist champions and assailing the northern financial and mercantile interests aligned with Hamilton … the national consensus

that the slavery issue should be tabled to preserve the union meant that the southern plantation economy was effectively ruled off-limits to political discussion, while Hamilton's system, by default, underwent the most searching scrutiny.

In order to deflect attention from the morality of slavery, Southern representatives cast the debate in terms of regional economics, claiming that slavery was inherently Southern and an agricultural necessity, in the same way manufacturing and commerce was necessary to the North. Therefore, the abolitionist movement was the Northern states' way of attempting to dominate the South—and urban businessmen's way of dominating the rural farmer. This line of argument had major repercussions. In the short term, it threw a ghastly light on Hamilton's plan for growing the government through banking and trade. It also imbued the next century with conflict between the North and South, where the Northern states would repeatedly scold the South for bad behavior while the Southern states accused the Northern states of plotting to overpower them. This conflict led to the Civil War in 1861.

The disintegration of the Union was one of Hamilton's greatest fears and one of the leading reasons he sought to grow the power of the federal government into one unifying body that would hold the states together. Though Hamilton was known for his staunch objection to slavery, he bit his tongue through this debate, throwing his weight behind his national plan instead. Even this strategy backfired, as southerners believed a larger national government could more easily strong-arm them into abolishing slavery.

Hamilton's decision not to speak out regarding abolition at this time was a rare moment of self-restraint. Historians suspect he couldn't bite his tongue long and attribute an article that appeared the following year under the name "Civis" to the secretary of the treasury. In this article, the author reproached Southern representatives for guarding their personal interests over the needs of their citizens,

An issue of both morality and economics, the use of slavery was debated often and created deep ideological rifts between citizens and politicians alike.

and alluded to Jefferson and Madison specifically, writing that those most vocal about liberty held the bill of rights in one hand and a whip for slaves in the other.

A Compromise

Leading up to the debate on assuming state debt, the location of the nation's capital had also been under discussion. The temporary capital had been in New York City, though the members of the Constitutional Convention had decided that the capital should be set apart from any state.

During the early years following the revolution, members of the Continental Army, which had been formed by the Second Continental Congress to fight against the British, threatened Congress with violence, claiming they had not been paid for their services. Congressional delegates had thus been chased from state to state, starting in Philadelphia. When Pennsylvania refused to call the local militia to protect Congress against these soldiers, they decided the capital could not be at the mercy of any single state government and thus wrote the provision into the Constitution for a ten-mile plot of land where Congress would be located.

The most extreme critics, such as Governor Clinton, saw this plan as the federal government's attempt to create an elitist territory where officials would fritter away their time in office in the lap of exorbitant luxury. More common was the fear that though the provision for the new capital removed it from any one state, the surrounding states would benefit disproportionally from their proximity to the nation's seat of power. Additionally, a temporary capital was needed while the permanent one was being built.

Rather than gaining influence, Hamilton's strong desire to keep the capital in New York, at least temporarily, was working against his plans for the nation's finances. His identity was becoming so enmeshed with that of New York City that it was seen as representing his home turf, which other members of state were beginning to resent and fight against. Because of the distribution of members of the House and Senate, Virginia had a disproportionate number of representatives, many of whom had lost interest in traveling by horse and carriage to New York. Naturally, under threat of abolition, they also wanted the additional influence of establishing the seat of national government in the South.

Under attacks for his financial report and with the time to vote on his plan drawing near, Hamilton met with Jefferson and Madison in one of the most famous meals of American history. Jefferson hosted the party and agreed with Hamilton that assuming state debt would unify the states and maintain good credit abroad. Madison countered that assuming state debt put states that had none, such as Virginia, into the position of paying for more delinquent states. He would only be willing to take on that responsibility if Virginia would receive something in return.

Thus, Hamilton agreed to support a temporary capital in Philadelphia and a permanent capital on the Potomac River, if they would support his plans for dealing with the debt and the national bank. Though Hamilton, Jefferson, and Madison had negotiated an amicable solution with which many members of Congress would agree, the privacy of their discussion smacked of corruption. The bargain was also unpopular with New Yorkers, and while there is no guarantee that Hamilton could have persuaded the other states to keep the capital in his city, the relocation of the government has surely had a lasting effect on America.

Uncontestable Brilliance

Despite fierce opposition to many of his proposals, Hamilton was able to push through an astounding majority of his financial plans and his interpretation of the Constitution. As a result of his work, which proved almost alarmingly successful, many detractors were forced to eat their words.

In their book on the establishment of early American finance, Robert E. Wright and David J. Cowen wrote:

> The positive effects of funding and assumption of the debt upon not only the country's credit standing but also its commerce were felt almost immediately. Writing from Hartford in 1791, Noah Webster, the "schoolmaster of America," boasted about the era of prosperity brought on by assumption. "The establishment of funds to maintain public credit … has an amazing effect upon the face of business and the country. Commerce … revives and the country is full of provision. Manufactures are increasing to a great degree, and in the large towns vast improvements are making in pavements and buildings."

Hamilton had successfully not only spurred on the new American economy but provided an era of prosperity and confidence in government. Due to his work, the early union would be preserved. In addition to this, Hamilton's fame was secured—and news of his accomplishments traveled across the ocean to Europe.

Alexander Hamilton accepted the massive responsibility of secretary of treasury at just thirty-four years old. It was simultaneously an enormous honor and an invitation for conflict. No one in the new republic could have been as qualified for the job as Hamilton—his firsthand knowledge of the expense of operating a military on the national level, his experience opening a bank, and his intimate knowledge of imports and exports from the West Indies made him uniquely suited to the position. Just as importantly, Hamilton had the confidence to stick to his principles and fight for his vision of the new nation, made up of individual states connected through a strong federal government.

Copyright, 1876, by Currier & Ives N.Y.

GEN! HENRY KNOX, Secy. of War.

ALEXANDER HAMILTON. Secy. of the Treasury.

THOMAS JEFFERSON Secy. of State.

GEORGE WASHINGTON.

EDMUND RANDOLPH, Attorney General.

WASHINGTON AND HIS CABINET.

Hamilton joined Washington's cabinet as the first Secretary of the Treasury at just thirty-four years old, but few would have been up to the challenges that position entailed.

CHAPTER SIX

Alexander Hamilton's Lasting Legacy

Perhaps because he didn't live to write his own version of history, Hamilton is as well known for his death in a duel as for his massive contributions to American government. Hamilton's famous duel against Aaron Burr in 1804 was the result of mounting tensions between Hamilton and his colleagues in politics. Hamilton distrusted Burr, having at different times throughout his career questioned his colleague's scruples. When Burr ran for president against Thomas Jefferson, Hamilton set aside his differences with Jefferson in the interest of defeating his more contentious rival. The race for president had been so close that Hamilton intimated to others that he found Burr corrupt and unprincipled. Though he may have been correct on many counts, it was his dogged

As with many of the Founding Fathers, Americans today regularly enjoy Hamilton's contribution to their government without realizing it. Hamilton's portrait on the ten-dollar bill is a regular reminder of the man who dedicated his life to creating a strong central government and economy.

commitment to principle that entangled him in a mess from which he would never emerge, leaving others to recreate the events of his life in his absence.

The Foundation of a Myth

At a private dinner party, Hamilton lamented to his host that Aaron Burr might run for governor of New York. One guest recounted the incident to a friend in a letter, claiming, broadly, that Hamilton found Burr "despicable." That letter was subsequently printed in a local newspaper.

Burr had just suffered a series of embarrassing political defeats and was particularly sensitive to insult. Though he had quietly ignored Hamilton's conduct over the previous few years, either in the interest of maintaining peace (as he claimed) or because Hamilton was too popular and powerful to challenge (as historian Ron Chernow suggests), Burr could not let this public insult go unpunished. In fact, Burr seems to have been hoping for an opportunity to duel to regain some of his honor, lost as it was over the course of his political career.

On June 27, 1804, Burr sent the formal request for a duel. Though it was customary to arrange a duel for the immediate future, Hamilton postponed the event until July 11 so he could be certain to meet professional obligations on July 6. Even facing the possibility of his own death, Hamilton's sense of responsibility and pride were unsullied. This postponement also made for strange interaction between the rivals, who still moved in the same social circles and were friendly enough with one another that friends did not know anything was amiss.

All manner of speculation has been made on Hamilton's apparent desire to engage in a mortal duel. After recent political backslides it's possible that Hamilton had fallen into a deep depression and saw the duel as assisted suicide, allowing him to die with honor that, if jeopardized, he would not be able to aid his country without. It is also possible that he knew rather than saving Burr's career, killing

Hamilton, who still enjoyed many admirers in the public, would ensure Burr's own political death. Either way, Hamilton refused to listen to the reason of his friends and entered the duel on his own, perhaps misguided, terms.

Hamilton's son, Philip, had been seen as a natural politician with a strong mind, ready to follow in his father's footsteps. He'd gone to his own duel to spare his honor but with the conviction that it would be wrong to kill. Philip was committed to firing an errant shot rather than aim at his opponent. This choice cost him his life. Unfortunately, Hamilton followed in the footsteps of his son.

As for the nation Hamilton left in his wake, its citizens were devastated by this great man's senseless death. Though he was never president himself, he was bid farewell by a grieving nation.

A New Nation

It's impossible to know what America would look like today without the massive influence of Alexander Hamilton. From his early pamphlets and his bravery during the revolution to his dogged support of the Constitution and his superhuman abilities in laying out the financial foundation of the American government, Hamilton's vision of the new nation has undoubtedly shaped American culture today.

In support of this idea, biographer Chernow suggests that Alexander Hamilton's increased popularity today is due, in part, to his ability to predict what the future of America would look like:

> Hamilton had a very modern take on our economic future. He envisioned a country built on banks, corporations, stock exchanges and factories. This was a frightening and sinister vision to a lot of Americans at the time. Jefferson represented a more soothing point of view: an America of small towns and traditional agriculture. I think one reason for the eventual reappraisal of Hamilton is that

A NOTE ON DUELING

In the early nineteenth century, dueling was not a common ritual of honor. Some of the Founding Fathers eschewed dueling as barbarian and senseless, though the practice was most common among politicians, many of whom had military backgrounds and romanticized the idea of dying for honor. Both Hamilton and Burr were military men, and Hamilton's incessant longing to be in the battle's fray throughout the revolution foreshadowed his readiness for a death that brought with it dignity and courage. Yet even as he felt compelled to follow through, there were many reasons that Hamilton would have second thoughts. His son, Philip, had died in a duel only a few years before, and Hamilton's last speech had condemned dueling.

Hamilton may have taken solace in the fact that the point of dueling was rarely to kill one's opponent. Often the duel could be avoided all together with the aid of moderators, called seconds, who came to the event with the offended parties. If the quarrel could not be resolved without violence, the offended parties would face off and shoot, but aim for an arm or leg, rather than a deathly blow. Perhaps these norms gave Hamilton the illusion of safety.

America has grown into the contours of the country of his imagination, not Jefferson's. We have caught up to his prophetic vision.

Hamilton's vision helped shape America—but he also had the ability to understand how American society would evolve. The United States today bears little resemblance to the country that Hamilton knew, but this Founding Father's work still influences our contemporary political and economic systems to this day.

The Arts

Alexander Hamilton's recent uptick in popularity in the wake of Chernow's biography has lent his legacy to a wide array of artistic interpretations, some more reverent than others.

Perhaps most notable among these endeavors is Lin-Manuel Miranda's Broadway musical, simply titled *Hamilton*, which debuted on the Great White Way in September 2015 after a groundbreakingly successful off-Broadway run. Miranda composed, wrote the lyrics to, and acted in the title role of the show. Far from a dry retelling of facts, *Hamilton* is an intense, sung-through performance complete with political rap battles and nationalist pop breakup ballads. In a surprising reimagining of the Founding Fathers, the cast is as racially diverse as the music. Miranda says of the musical, "This is the story of America then, told by America now—it looks like America now."

Depicting the story of Hamilton's rise to fame and his battles with Burr, Jefferson, Madison, and Adams, the show has played to sold-out audiences and received high praise from viewers, the media, and President Barack Obama alike.

The young, tenacious Founding Father has also captured the imagination of visual artists for centuries. Sculptures of the secretary of treasury can be found in cities across the country from New York, New York, to Cleveland, Ohio, including a pair of life-sized statues at the New York Historical Society representing Hamilton and Burr with pistols raised. Independent artists have also reimagined

Hamilton, the Broadway musical by Lin-Manuel Miranda, brings the story of young, visionary Hamilton to the stage with a message about the contributions of immigrants and rebels to the American dream that is still relevant today.

Hamilton in a variety of ways. An artist who borrows Hamilton's pen name for his drawings, Publius-Reported, has illustrated Hamilton in every scenario from Pokémon trainer to retro pin-up girl.

Financial Legacy

There's a reason Alexander Hamilton was honored with a place on American currency. As secretary of the treasury, it is no surprise that Hamilton's legacy is in relation to the financial systems in the United

States. While he made many other contributions as a lawyer, writer, and abolitionist, it is the many financial theories and plans he laid out for the nation for which he is remembered.

The Central Bank

When Hamilton became secretary of the treasury, the new nation was bankrupt from the Revolutionary War. Hamilton understood that, in order for America to become a stable country, its debt needed to be reduced and its economy built up—and he was instrumental in helping it to do just that. According to Chernow, "[Hamilton] provided the country with an economic and financial maturity that enabled it to give the Constitution and federal government a fair test."

Possibly the crowning jewel in Hamilton's vision for what America could become was the creation of the national bank. In 1831, Daniel Webster, an American senator, gave a speech in New York celebrating Hamilton's contribution to American government, saying:

> He smote the rock of the national resources, and abundant streams of revenue gushed forth. He touched the dead corpse of the Public Credit, and it sprung upon its feet. The fabled birth of Minerva, from the brain of Jove, was hardly more sudden or more perfect than the financial system of the United States, as it burst forth from the conceptions of Alexander Hamilton.

But as the adamant disapproval from his contemporaries implies, the central bank has not always enjoyed such celebration. When the bank's charter expired after twenty years, Congress did not renew it, and Hamilton wasn't there to defend the bank. Five years later, amid a struggle to finance the War of 1812, James Madison reinstated the bank, hoping to put the American currency's rapid inflation back in check. When Andrew Jackson took over as president in 1828, he

GENERAL JACKSON SLAYING THE MANY HEADED MONSTER.

This political cartoon from 1836 mocks President Andrew Jackson's attack on the national bank, which was supported by state banks. Each head of the snake represents one of the states, and Jackson is aided in his crusade by Martin Van Buren and Jack Downing.

dissolved the bank yet again, believing that speculation on bonds as a way to generate revenue was corrupt and unstable. This bold move was to the chagrin of many Americans who feared inflation would again wreak havoc on the economy. Indeed, inflation was quickly on the rise and, to bring it back under control, Jackson mandated that all federal debt would be paid with gold and silver.

Additionally, the Michigan Act of 1837 lowered supervision of new state banks. As a result, state banks began taking over the role of the national bank, and small banks proliferated throughout the country. These banks were less stable, however, and often closed after only a few years because they were unable to pay back the value of the bonds they sold, which often lost value. This was known as the Free

Banking Era. In 1863, as America entered the Civil War, the National Banking Act was passed to provide funds for the war, to create a system of national banks that would be more rigorous and trustworthy than the state banks, and to create a uniform national currency.

The Panic of 1907 had an interesting effect on national banking. Though the Founding Fathers had feared corruption from greedy bankers and speculators, employees at small banks grew concerned that large private bankers were forming a monopoly in 1907, and demanded more government oversight and control over the elasticity of national wealth. Over the next fifty years, the Federal Reserve Bank emerged in response to this concern. In the 1970s, Congress charged the Federal Reserve Bank with the responsibility of securing stable employment, prices, and interest rates.

Author John Steele Gordon reports that "the national debt that Hamilton began with a bank loan of $19,608.81 is the largest single entry on any set of books in the world. [Today] the federal government pays $19,608.81 in interest on its current debt every 2.4 seconds."

There is no question about the difference of scale between Hamilton's national bank and its modern equivalent—America is a larger country with a larger government and larger bills, just as Hamilton predicted it would be—and Hamilton's vision is surprisingly intact. Today, the Federal Reserve Bank regulates smaller banks and maintains financial stability for the entire country. One of Hamilton's highest goals was to encourage national unity through economic stability, and the founding of a federal bank is one of the primary reasons America has been able to recover from national economic disasters like the Great Depression in the 1920s and the Great Recession in 2008.

Slavery

Hamilton's view on slavery was exceptional. He fought for American freedom from the British and Tory freedom from American

Hamilton College was born from the Hamilton-Oneida Academy, which Hamilton helped found to educate both whites and Natives in support of good relations between these two often-clashing groups.

reactionaries, and he maintained that blacks and whites were not just hypothetically equal, but genetically equal. Even some of the most ardent supporters of emancipation, including Thomas Jefferson, questioned the intellectual capacity of blacks. Having been born and raised on a predominantly black island, Hamilton was convinced of true equality among American citizens regardless of race.

His vision of freedom and liberty for all also extended to Native Americans. Unlike many of his contemporaries, politicians and citizens alike, Hamilton championed good relations with the native tribes and eschewed the violence against them on the western frontier. He even chartered a new school in Western New York, the Hamilton-Oneida Academy, to educate both whites and natives in English and tribal languages. The school later became Hamilton College. Such an enlightened approach proves Hamilton's penchant for communication above coercion.

In particular, the legacy of the slavery debate has been far-reaching—from early economic concerns to the Civil War and the civil rights movement—and is deeply intertwined with the foundation of American government.

As a result of the ongoing struggle between north and south over slavery raging on, this debate made popular the vilification of business and manufacturing as un-American. Through this scheme, the southern representatives created an enduring narrative that business was the enemy of agriculture, that the elite aristocrats who ran these businesses would soon return the government to a new monarchy by a different name—never mind that the slaveholders themselves were enormously wealthy and practiced the most ruthless form of tyranny of all: slavery.

Vestiges of these tensions can be seen in the rhetoric of politicians today, who still seek to align themselves with the working class. By presenting their opponents as elitist and favoring foreign diplomacy over domestic issues, equally wealthy candidates endear themselves to the large, lower-income populace.

Constitutional Interpretation

Jefferson's rejection of Hamilton's bank has had long-lasting consequences—not just for Hamilton's proposal, but for the way the Constitution would be interpreted moving forward. Hamilton believed that the Constitution's strength was its sometimes vague language, used by the authors to allow for growth and change. It is actually a huge testament to the brilliance of those who contributed to the document that they were not blinded by their present situation and were able to leave room for inevitable change. Today, there is still heated debate between "originalists" who support following the original Constitution to the letter, and "progressives" who, perhaps ironically, see the Constitution as the original founding fathers saw it—a flexible document that was capable of serving the people, not the other way around. In fact, one of the deepest fears

Hamilton's return to New York City after his tireless campaign to ratify the Constitution was celebrated with a parade, including a float in the shape of a large battleship bearing his name.

of early Americans was putting into place a government incapable of growing to meet the potential of its citizens.

Perhaps Hamilton's greatest contribution to American history is no more than this interpretation of the Constitution. Jefferson had averred that Hamilton's national bank bill was unconstitutional because it was not written explicitly into the Constitution. Hamilton's legal experience played a huge role in his ability to convince his peers that the new government was bestowed with **implied powers**, that is, that the Constitution bestowed the government with the power to do whatever they deemed necessary, except where explicitly stated otherwise.

The American public celebrated Hamilton when he returned to New York after his tireless campaign to ratify the Constitution— the symbol of a country he dedicated his life to building. And, today, the American government remains a testament to Hamilton's vision of united states, joined together under the federal government, to preserve the rights and freedoms of all their citizens.

CHRONOLOGY

1755 Scholars believe Alexander Hamilton was born on April 11.

1757 Alexander Hamilton claims this as his birth year.

1766 Hamilton impresses wealthy locals and wins their favor.

1770 The Boston Massacre contributes to growing unrest in the colonies.

1773 Hamilton is sent to King's College by wealthy benefactors.

1774 The first Continental Congress issues its Declarations and Resolves; Hamilton writes "A Full Vindication of the Measures of Congress."

1775 The American Revolution begins at the battle of Lexington and Concord; King's College closes, and Hamilton joins the war.

1776 The Declaration of Independence is signed.

1777 Hamilton's military skill gains the attention of General George Washington; Hamilton is promoted from captain to lieutenant colonel.

1779 Hamilton writes to the Continental Congress to ask that slaves be admitted to the military and that they receive their freedom in exchange.

1780 Hamilton marries Elizabeth Schuyler.

1782 Hamilton begins practicing law in New York; he travels to Philadelphia as New York's representative to the Continental Congress.

1783 The Treaty of Paris officially ends the revolution.

1784 Hamilton helps create the Bank of New York and advocates for Tories' rights.

1785 Hamilton helps form the New York Society for Promoting the Manumission of Slaves.

1787 Hamilton attends the Second Continental Congress; he writes the *Federalist Papers* alongside John Jay and James Madison in support of centralized government.

1789 Hamilton is elected secretary of the treasury under President George Washington.

1795 Hamilton retires from his post as secretary of the treasury and returns to practicing law.

1798 Hamilton is elected inspector general of the army.

1800 Hamilton retires from the army.

1804 Hamilton dies after receiving a gunshot wound in a duel with Vice President Aaron Burr.

GLOSSARY

abolitionists Those people who opposed slavery in the United States.

Albany Plan A plan proposed by Benjamin Franklin in 1745 to unite the thirteen colonies.

approbation Approval or praise.

Articles of Confederation Signed by the thirteen colonies to assert their power as sovereign and unified states, this document served as the first constitution of the United States of America.

assimilate To create a likeness between two disparate things or ideas.

Benjamin Franklin A Founding Father, ambassador, inventor, and printer.

Boston Massacre An unplanned fight between a patriot mob and British soldiers in Boston, Massachusetts, on March 5, 1770.

Boston Tea Party A political protest in Boston resulting in the destruction of 300 pounds of tea (136 kg) and strict trade embargoes from England.

British West Indies Presently referred to as the British Overseas Territories, this land includes the Caribbean, Anguilla, Bermuda, Cayman Islands, and Montserrat.

Coercive Acts Punitive legislation issued in response to the Boston Tea Party.

Committee of Correspondence A system of communication organized by patriot leaders as the American Revolution approached.

"Common Sense" A pamphlet written by Thomas Paine credited with convincing the American colonists to break free of British rule.

conciliations Compromises used to persuade Britain to lessen their strict taxes and regulations on the American colonies so as to avoid war.

Continental Congress An early version of the American government in which delegates from the thirteen original colonies convened to create unity among the colonies. It met in three iterations between 1774 and 1789.

Currency Act British legislation forbidding the American colonists from printing their own money.

Declaration of Independence A document ratified on July 4, 1776, declaring the United States of America as a sovereign nation independent of British rule.

ennui Boredom.

Federalist Papers A series of fifty-eight essays intended to convince the public to ratify the constitution; the essays were composed by Alexander Hamilton, James Madison, and John Jay.

French and Indian War The North American conflict between British American colonies and France and its Native American allies for westward expansion, from 1754 to 1763.

General Thomas Gage The British Military Governor in Massachusetts leading up to the American Revolution.

intolerance An unwillingness to compromise.

implied powers Powers of government neither explicitly granted or denied by the Constitution.

John Hancock Cofounder of the Massachusetts Committee of Correspondence with Samuel Adams, who provided financial support for the distribution of reports to other colonies.

mercantilism Establishing a relationship between merchants and a government so ensure mutual benefits.

Paul Revere Freedom rider and American spy.

revolutionary Tending to, promoting, or involving revolution.

Quartering Act British legislation requiring colonists to feed and house British troops.

Samuel Adams Cofounder of the Massachusetts Committee of Correspondence with John Hancock. Wrote many bulletins distributed by freedom riders across the colonies.

Seven Years' War The ongoing conflict between Britain and France from 1756–1763, of which The French and Indian War was a part.

smuggling The illegal import or export of goods from one country to another.

specious Superficially beautiful or attractive but not so in reality.

Stamp Act A British tax placed on printed documents in the colonies.

Thomas Hutchinson Prominent loyalist politician and Governor of Massachusetts.

Thomas Paine Revolutionary thinker and author of "Common Sense."

Tea Act British use of mercantilism to establish taxation of the American colonies through the East India Tea Company.

SOURCES

CHAPTER ONE

pg. 11: Franklin, Benjamin. *The Pennsylvania Gazette*, May 9, 1754.

pg. 15: "American Revolution," Library of Congress. Accessed December 5, 2015, www.loc.gov/teachers/classroommaterials/presentationsandactivities/presentations/timeline/amrev/rebelln.

pg. 26: Letter from John Adams to Abigail Adams, 3 July 1776, "Had a Declaration..." [electronic edition]. *Adams Family Papers: An Electronic Archive*. Massachusetts Historical Society. Accessed December 14, 2015, www.masshist.org/digitaladams.

CHAPTER TWO

pg. 38: Chernow, Ron, *Hamilton*, e-book edition. Accessed December 26, 2015, epubbookonline.com/b/3449/ron-chernow/alexander-hamilton/6.

pg. 43: Chernow, *Hamilton*, p. 484.

pg. 43-44: Hamilton, Alexander and Aaron Burr, *Hamilton-Burr Duel Correspondences*, Wikisource. Accessed December 27, 2015. en.wikisource.org/wiki/Hamilton%E2%80%93Burr_duel_correspondences.

pg. 45: Valley Forge Historical Society, www.ushistory.org/valleyforge/served/hamilton.html.

CHAPTER THREE

pg. 50: Chernow, Ron, *Hamilton*, p. 688.

pg. 50: *Ibid.*, p. 716.

pg. 50: *Ibid.*, p. 717.

pg. 51: "Jefferson to Benjamin Rush, September 23, 1800," in *PTJ*, 32:168, Founders Online, Accessed December 31, 2015, founders.archives.gov/documents/Jefferson/01-32-02-0102.

pg. 56: For all quotations from the *Federalist Papers*, The Avalon Project at Yale Law School has been used. Site last updated 2008. Accessed December 26, 2015, avalon.law.yale.edu/18th_century/fed01.asp.

pg. 56: "Father of the Constitution," James Madison's Montpelier, www.montpelier.org/james-and-dolley-madison/james-madison/father-of-the-constitution.

pg. 56: Franklin, Ben, "Madison Debate," September 17,1787. avalon.law.yale.edu/18th_century/debates_917.asp#2.

pg. 57: "James Madison," The White House. Accessed December 11, 2015, www.whitehouse.gov/1600/presidents/jamesmadison.

pgs. 58-59: Paine, Thomas, "Common Sense," *US History*. Accessed December 11, 2015, www.ushistory.org/paine/commonsense/sense1.htm.

CHAPTER FOUR

pgs. 62-63: Hamilton, Alexander, "A Full Vindication of the Measures of Congress." Accessed December 20, 2015, oll.libertyfund.org/titles/2121.

pg. 65: Chernow, *Hamilton*, p. 195.

pg. 68: Chernow, *Hamilton*, p. 260.

pgs. 72-73: Hamilton, Alexander, "Report on Public Credit." Accessed December 16, 2015, oll.libertyfund.org/titles/2121.

pgs. 76-77: Hamilton, Alexander, "National Bank Excerpts." Accessed December 20, 2015, www.gilderlehrman.org/sites/default/files/inline-pdfs/Hamilton%20on%20National%20Bank%20excerpts.pdf.

CHAPTER FIVE

pg. 80: Chernow, *Hamilton*, p. 171.

pgs. 87-88: Sherman, Rodger, "Alexander Hamilton's Financial Program," 1790. Accessed December 22, 2015, www.digitalhistory.uh.edu/disp_textbook.cfm?smtID=3&psid=268.

pg. 88: Jefferson, Thomas, The Founders' Constitution. Volume 3, Article 1, Section 8, Clause 18, Document 10, The University of Chicago Press. Accessed December 10, 2015. press-pubs.uchicago.edu/founders/documents/a1_8_18s10.html.

pg. 89: Chernow, *Hamilton*, p. 301.

pgs. 89-90: *Ibid.*, p. 211.

pg. 94: Wright, Robert E. and Cowen, David J., "Financial Founding Fathers: The Men Who Made America Rich," 2006. Accessed Dec 22, 2015, www.press.uchicago.edu/Misc/Chicago/910687.html.

CHAPTER SIX

pg. 99: Zoglin, Richard, "Interview with Ron Chernow," *Time*, December 30, 2015. Accessed December 31st, 2015, time. com/4149352/ron-chernow-alexander-hamilton-interview.

pg. 101: Mead, Rebecca, "All About the Hamiltons," *The New Yorker*, February 9, 2015. Accessed January 11, 2016, www. newyorker.com/magazine/2015/02/09/hamiltons.

pg. 103: Zoglin, "Interview with Ron Chernow."

pg. 103: *Respectfully Quoted: A Dictionary of Quotations Requested from the Congressional Research Service*. (Washington, DC: Library of Congress, 1989; Bartleby.com, 2003.) Accessed January 7, 2016, www.bartleby.com/73.

pg. 105: Gordon, John Steele, "Past & Present: Alexander Hamilton and the Start of the Nation," *US News*, September 18, 2008. Accessed January 7, 2016, www.usnews.com/opinion/ articles/2008/09/18/past-present-alexander-hamilton-and-the-start-of-the-national-debt?page=2.

FURTHER INFORMATION

BOOKS

Adams, John and Abigail. *Letters of John and Abigail Adams*. New York: Start Publishing LLC, 2012.

Berkin, Carol. *Revolutionary Mothers: Women in the Struggle for American Independence*. New York: Vintage, 2007.

Chernow, Ron. *Washington: A Life*. New York: Penguin Books, 2010.

Gonick, Larry. *The Cartoon History of the United States*. Dunmore, PA: William Morrow Paperbacks, 1991.

Paine, Thomas. *The Writings of Thomas Paine*. New York: The Library of America, 1995.

WEBSITES

The Grange
www.nps.gov/hagr/index.htm

The National Park Service runs The Grange, the only house Hamilton ever owned. Built shortly before his death, it was restored in 2008 and is open to the public.

It's Hamilton Time
www.itshamiltime.com

This witty blog regularly posts interesting facts and documents related to Alexander Hamilton, including original correspondence by and about him, as well as comparisons to modern interpretations of historical events involving the first Secretary of the Treasury.

Library of Congress
www.loc.gov

This invaluable resource hosts a plethora of information. The Library of Congress was the nation's first cultural institution and the physical space is the largest library in the world. Much of their catalog, including film, art, government documents and much more, is available on this website.

MUSEUMS

Hamilton Grange
414 West 141st Street
New York, NY 10031

National Constitution Center
525 Arch Street
Philadelphia, PA 19106

National Museum of American History
14th Street and Constitution Avenue, NW
Washington, DC 20001

BIBLIOGRAPHY

Adams Family Papers: An Electronic Archive. Massachusetts Historical Society. Accessed December 14, 2015. www. masshist.org/digitaladams.

"Albany Plan of Union, 1754." US Department of State: Office of the Historian. Accessed January 12, 2016. history.state.gov/ milestones/1750-1775/albany-plan.

"The American Revolution, 1763–1783." Library of Congress. Accessed December 5, 2015 www.loc.gov/teachers/ classroommaterials/presentationsandactivities/presentations/ timeline/amrev/rebelln.

Chernow, Ron. *Alexander Hamilton.* E-book edition. epubbookonline.com/b/3449/ron-chernow/alexander-hamilton.

C.W., and A.J.K.D. "Did Slavery Make Economic Sense?" *The Economist*, September 27, 2013. Accessed January 12, 2016. http://www.economist.com/blogs/freeexchange/2013/09/ economic-history-2.

"The Federalist Papers." The Avalon Project at Yale Law School. Accessed December 26, 2015. avalon.law.yale.edu/18th_ century/fed01.asp.

Franklin, Benjamin. "Madison Debates, September 17, 1787." Accessed December 16, 2015. avalon.law.yale.edu/18th_ century/debates_917.asp#2.

Freidel, Frank, and Hugh Sidney. "James Madison." The White House. Accessed January 12, 2016. www.whitehouse.gov/1600/presidents/jamesmadison.

Gonick, Larry. *The Cartoon History of the United States*. New York: HarperPerennial, 1991.

Gordon, John Steele. "Past & Present: Alexander Hamilton and the Start of the National Debt." *US News*, September 18, 2008. Accessed January 7, 2016 www.usnews.com/opinion/articles/2008/09/18/past-present-alexander-hamilton-and-the-start-of-the-national-debt?.

Hamilton, Alexander. "A Full Vindication of the Measures of Congress." Accessed December 20, 2015. oll.libertyfund.org/titles/2121.

Hamilton, Alexander, and Burr, Aaron. "Hamilton-Burr Duel Correspondences." Wikisource. Accessed December 27, 2015 en.wikisource.org/wiki/Hamilton%E2%80%93Burr_duel_correspondences.

Hamilton, Alexander. "The Papers of Alexander Hamilton," ed. Harold Syrett et al. (New York and London: Columbia University Press, 1963), 7:305–342.

———. "Report on Public Credit." Accessed December 16, 2015 oll.libertyfund.org/titles/2121.

———. "The Revolutionary Writings of Alexander Hamilton," Richard B. Vernier, ed. (Indianapolis: Liberty Fund, 2008). 11/2/2015. oll.libertyfund.org/titles/2121.

———. *Writings*. Joanne B. Freedman, ed. New York: Library of America, 2001.

Heyrman, Christine Leigh. "Religion and the American Revolution." TeacherServe, National Humanities Center. nationalhumanitiescenter.org/tserve/eighteen/ekeyinfo/erelrev.htm.

"James Madison's Contribution to the Constitution." America's Story from America's Library. Accessed January 12, 2016. www.americaslibrary.gov/aa/madison/aa_madison_father_1.html.

Jefferson to Benjamin Rush, September 23, 1800, in PTJ, 32:168. Accessed December 31, 2015. Transcription available at Founders Online.

Jefferson, Thomas. The Founders' Constitution. Volume 3, Article 1, Section 8, Clause 18, Document 10 The University of Chicago Press. Accessed December 10, 2015. press-pubs.uchicago.edu/founders/documents/a1_8_18s10.html.

Lepore, Jill. "The Commandments." The *New Yorker*. January 17, 2011. Accessed January 12, 2016. www.newyorker.com/magazine/2011/01/17/the-commandments.

Letter from John Adams to Abigail Adams, 3 July 1776, "Had a Declaration ...".

Marrin, Albert. *The War for Independence: The Story of the American Revolution*. New York: Atheneum, 1988.

Mead, Rebecca. "A Hip-Hop Interpretation of the Founding Fathers." The *New Yorker*. February 9, 2015. Accessed January 12, 2016. www.newyorker.com/magazine/2015/02/09/hamiltons.

Paine, Thomas. "Common Sense." Ushistory.org. Accessed January 12, 2016. www.ushistory.org/paine/commonsense/sense1.htm.

Provincial Congress. *A Narrative, of the excursion and ravages of the King's troops under the command of General Gage, on the nineteenth of April, 1775. Together with the depositions taken by order of Congress, to support the truth of it.* Published by authority (Worcester: Isaiah Thomas, 1775), 19.

Respectfully Quoted: A Dictionary of Quotations Requested from the Congressional Research Service. Washington D.C.: Library of Congress, 1989; Bartleby.com, 2003. Accessed January 7, 2016. www.bartleby.com/73.

Sherman, Rodger. "Alexander Hamilton's Financial Programs." Digital History. Accessed December 22, 2015. www.digitalhistory.uh.edu/disp_textbook.cfm?smtID=3.

"Timeline: Alexander Hamilton Chronology." PBS. August 5, 2007. Accessed January 12, 2016. www.pbs.org/wgbh/amex/hamilton/timeline.

Wright, Robert E. and David J. Cowen. "Financial Founding Fathers: The Men Who Made America Rich." 2006. Accessed Dec 22, 2015 http://www.press.uchicago.edu/Misc/Chicago/910687.html.

Zoglin, Richard. "Interview with Ron Chernow," *Time*, December 30, 2015. Accessed December 31, 2015. time.com/4149352/ron-chernow-alexander-hamilton-interview.

INDEX

Page numbers in **boldface** are illustrations. Entries in **boldface** are glossary terms.

national bank, 7, 72–73,
   74–75, 76–77, 88, 93,
   103–105, 109

Paine, Thomas, 58–59, **59**
Parliament, 5, 12–13, 16–17,
   21, 63
Princeton, 32, 54
printing press, 18
Publius, 66, 68

Quartering Act, 12

religion, 10, 45, 59
Report on Public Credit, 72
Revere, Paul, 17–18, 22
revolutionary, 33–34, 38,
   58–59

Second Continental
   Congress, 23–24
Secretary of Treasury, 7, 39,
   67, 71, 79, 94, 101
Seven Years' War, 12
slavery, 31, 51, 53, 63, 73, 86,
   89–90, **91**, 105, 107
smuggling, 10, 72
Sons of Liberty, 33, 62
Spain, 9, 24–25, 27
specious, 67

Stamp Act, 12–13
Stevens, Thomas, 31

taxation without
   representation, 5, 12–15, 17
Tea Act, 15
Tories, 25, 33, 40, 64–65

War of 1812, 57, 103
Washington, George, 7,
   16–17, 24, 27, 35–39, 37,
   42, 51, 58, 64, 68, 71, 77,
   78, 83, **95**

ABOUT THE AUTHOR

Tatiana Ryckman is a writer, editor, and teacher. She holds a bachelor's degree in journalism and a master's degree in creative writing. Other books by Tatiana include a biography of Oprah Winfrey, *Oprah Winfrey: Media Mogul and Philanthropist*; a novella, *Ancestry of Objects*; and a collection of short stories, *Twenty-Something*. Tatiana is currently collaborating on new projects with a visual artist and dancer. When she is not writing, she enjoys reading and bicycling with friends in Austin, Texas.